Handling
Employment
for
Bosses & Supervisors

*Guidelines to Avoid
Employee Lawsuits,
With a Touch of Humor*

by
Geoffrey H. Hopper
Labor and Employment Attorney

Received highest independent rating in North America

Robert D. Reed Publishers • Bandon, OR

Robert D. Reed Publishers
P.O. Box 1992
Bandon, OR 97411
Phone: 541-347-9882 • Fax: -9883
E-mail: 4bobreed@msn.com
web site: www.rdrpublishers.com

Editors: **Terri Tanner** and **Cleone Lyvonne**
Cover Designer: **Geoffrey H. Hopper** and **Cleone Lyvonne**
Front Cover Cartoon: ©**Alexey Bannykh/Dreamstime.com**
Typesetter: **Barbara Kruger**

ISBN 978-1-931741-89-7

Library of Congress Control Number 2007904638

Manufactured, typeset and printed in the United States of America

First Printing 2007

DEDICATION

I would like to dedicate this book to my wonderful wife Lauralea and my three children, Shannon, Morgan and Lauryn Hopper, all of whom not only provide constant love and support, but also keep me very grounded. This book is also dedicated to my parents Herman and Lou Hopper, who taught me that the only person who never makes a mistake is the person that never does a damn thing.

ACKNOWLEDGMENTS

I would like to acknowledge in particular, literally thousands of clients that I have worked with over the years, whose unique situations, circumstances, and trials and tribulations provided to me the experience and education to formulate this book so as to hopefully allow others to avoid such problems.

Further I appreciate my office staff, and in particular Terri Tanner, for her time and effort in transcribing my hours upon hours of dictation for this book, and the numerous edits and rewrites as well. Further appreciation is extended to my clients, many who are my friends, as well as other personal friends and family members for their support and encouragement regarding the publication of this book.

Special appreciation is also extended to Cleone Lyvonne for her work with me regarding the cover as well as the editing, and of course to the literally tens of thousands of individuals who, over the last several decades, attended my seminars and shared with me their experience and insights, some of which I have been able to incorporate into this book.

I am also grateful for the volumes of quotations on the Internet and in books like *Uncle John's Bathroom Reader's Series*.

CONTENTS

DISCLAIMER

You really didn't think you were going to read a book written by a lawyer without having one of these, did you? The realities are that labor and employment matters can vary from state to state, country to country and circumstances to circumstances. There are specific nuances that can never be taken into consideration in one generalized book trying to address such a vast topic. Accordingly it is still always a good idea to consult with qualified legal counsel about your particular labor and/or employment matter.

INTRODUCTION

The primary purpose of this book is to help supervisors and bosses with some of your more common employment problems. Employees might also read this book, so as to obtain better insight as to their boss and supervisor's mindset. For clarification purposes, the term "bosses" refers to those supervisors who are at the executive level of a business and typically includes Owners, Presidents, and CEOs. The term "supervisor" refers to all other individuals who in any manner supervise one or more individuals in their place of work.

All too often, the ability to diplomatically and constructively supervise employees is assumed and not taught. Frequently this results in low morale, absenteeism, reduced productivity, attorney's fees, and/or litigation. The average jury verdict in wrongful termination and discrimination lawsuits (including attorney's fees) can run in the six- to seven-digit numbers. Accordingly, a supervisor's ignorance of employment and/or labor matters is often financially beneficial for the knowledgeable employee and catastrophic for the employer.

On a daily basis for approximately three decades as a labor/employment attorney, I have handled virtually every employment situation imaginable involving literally thousands of employees in the most litigious state in the United States (California).

This book provides suggestions and recommendations designed to address some of the more frequent employment matters that keep attorneys employed. Set forth are not only some legal but also practical suggestions, as well as a mix of psychology, common sense, and hopefully some humor, for not only the employers themselves, but also supervisors. In more than ninety percent of the lawsuits we have handled, a supervisor has also been named as a defendant and faced the very real possibility of losing his home because of employment litigation. Attorney's fees alone can easily run in the six-digit numbers. While there is no substitute for experience and advice of competent counsel, this book strives to be of some assistance in an area where little exists.

Those persons who are typically the best bosses or supervisors are those who enjoy their jobs. This too is not something you can learn from a book. The most successful bosses and supervisors understand the fundamental rule in handling all employment matters, which is that while it is acceptable to occasionally socialize with your employees, you never become friends with them. Further, you *always* treat your employees with dignity and *respect*. Besides being the right thing to do, such also allows you to keep your home. Good luck!

> Geoffrey H. Hopper
> Geoffrey H. Hopper & Associates, APC
> P. O. Box 7159
> Redlands, California 92375
> phone: (909) 798-9800
> facsimile: (909) 798-9002
> email: ghh@hopperlaw.com
> website: www.hopperlaw.com

> *"It is amazing what you can accomplish*
> *if you do not care who gets the credit."*
> —*Harry S. Truman*

> *"If you just set out to be liked, you would be prepared*
> *to compromise on anything at any time,*
> *and you would achieve nothing."*
> —*Margaret Thatcher*

Twenty-Three (23) Factors Causing Employment Problems

It has been my experience that there are several factors leading to employee problems (oftentimes overlooked by employers and supervisors). These include (in no particular order) the following:

(1) Lack of understanding that the expense of defending litigation regarding employment matters can frequently cost in excess of $150,000.00, even if the employer/supervisor wins the lawsuit. If you lose, jury verdicts can range in the six- to seven-digit numbers (see Sections 1.0 through 1.7).

(2) Failure to utilize one of the multitudes of *options* of handling employment problems besides termination of employment (see Section 2.0, Step #8).

(3) Failure to comply with applicable laws regarding *posting* employment information (see Section 2.0, Step #10).

(4) Failure to properly *educate* and train supervisors (in particular mid-management) regarding handling of employment matters (see Section 2.0, Step #12).

(5) Failure of supervisors to understand the fact that employment litigation is typically not only against the employers but also against the *supervisors personally* (see Section 1.0 and Section 1.3).

(6) Lack of understanding and/or knowledge regarding the *At-will Doctrine* of employment (see Section 2.0, Step #14).

(7) Lack of understanding of the fundamental principle that employees typically do not sue employers and/or supervisors whom they *respect* (see Section 2.0, Step #1).

(8) Lack of understanding that it makes good business sense to treat employees fairly (see the entire book).

(9) Lack of application and/or understanding of the *Golden Rule of Employment* (see Section 2.0, Step #27).

(10) Lack of application and/or understanding of *the Blue-Haired Lady Doctrine* (see Section 2.0, Step #2).

(11) Lack of having and/or following *standardized practices and procedures* regarding employees (see Section 2.0, Step #10).

(12) Lack of understanding and/or failure to utilize the defense of "*advice of counsel*" (see Section 2.0, Step #21).

(13) Lack of understanding and/or failure to make use of the *after-acquired-evidence doctrine* (see Section 2.0, Step #3).

(14) Failure to understand and/or lack of utilization of *insurance* options regarding employment matters (see Section 2.0, Step #23).

(15) Failure to properly *document* employees by way of personnel files and/or anticipated litigation files (see Section 2.0, Step #11 and 31).

(16) Failure to properly handle and/or conduct *investigations*, which oftentimes results in greater liability than the original problem itself (see Section 6.4).

(17) Failure to understand the *David vs. Goliath* mindset of jurors regarding employees vs. employers and supervisors (see Section 2.0, Step #13).

(18) Failure to understand the inherent *bias* of the media in favor of employees and against employers and also the proper handling of the media in such matters (see Sections 5.7 and 10.4).

(19) Failure to understand the advantages, let alone use the methods by which to require employees to *arbitrate* employment disputes (see Section 2.0, Step #13).

(20) Failure on the part of employers to set up their businesses so as to *reduce personal exposure* to employment litigation (see Section 9.0).

(21) Failure to understand the primary *purpose of the Human Resources Representatives* and their function in the work place (see Section 2.0, Step #26).

(22) Failure to understand the importance of providing an *enjoyable working environment* for the employee (see Section 2.0, Step #18).

(23) Failure to use *common sense* (see the entire book).

Brief History of Employment Law

Before you start nodding off as you review this section, it is somewhat helpful to have some understanding of the evolution of employment law, which tells you not only where employment law has been but also where it is going and how it will affect you in the future. Employment law, unlike most other law, is quite recent, having really exploded in the United States within the last forty to fifty years. Most other areas of law, including contract law, real estate law, criminal law, etc., literally go back to Roman times.

For the most part, the United States derived much of its employment law from England starting back at the beginning of the 1800s. Employment law is very analogous to a pendulum swinging from being favorable for employers to at times being favorable for employees. Back in the 1800s, it was most favorable toward employers in that this is the time frame when there were rarely any laws to protect the rights of employees. Millions of immigrants had come to the United States competing for relatively few jobs in some of the larger cities. Male employees were oftentimes putting in seventeen- and eighteen-hour days as much as seven days and nights a week. Females and also children were working the sweatshops, not really having any protections about limits on their work hours until 1936. Employees were dying of black lung disease in the coal mines, OSHA was more of a noise that one made when they sneezed as opposed to any type of an organization providing any type of protection for an employee's working environment, and sexual harassment was more of a fringe benefit.

As set forth more specifically under Step 14, in 1877 California adopted the "at will" doctrine, which made it clear that employers could terminate employees with or without cause and with or without notice; however, they could not terminate employees for an unlawful reason, even back in 1877. (Now most all states in the

United States are at-will states; however, other countries are a mix of at-will and for-cause jurisdiction.) As time went on, employees noticed that if one or two of them complained, they did not have much clout; but if a couple thousand of them complained, they had a whole lot more clout, and this is the "Geoff Hopper in Five Seconds version of the history of the formation of unions."

By the early 1900s unions formed and sent lobbyists to Washington, D.C., and the pendulum, which previously was very much in favor of employers, began to swing more and more in favor of employees. By 1954, in the United States a case was handed down entitled *Brown v. Board of Education* that established prohibitions against discrimination based on race. As time evolved, laws were further established prohibiting discrimination based on disability, pregnancy, race, sex, age, marital status, religion, sexual orientation, gender, and finally including whistle blowing, etc. In the United States the law provided then, as it does now, that you cannot discipline or terminate employees based on such protected classifications or any time employees exercise any lawful rights that they have.

Up until the 1960s, typically if employees were mistreated in said manner, they would sue for breach of contract. However, in the 1960s, California, leading the way, established that employees could now sue under tort law as opposed to contract law. A tort is a civil wrong (not a French pastry); examples of such include negligence cases, slip-and-fall cases, trespass cases, defamation cases, legal malpractice, medical malpractice, etc. In essence, it is a situation wherein an employee can sue an employer or sometimes his supervisor for wrongful conduct as opposed to a breach of contract. You may say, "Who cares?" But the reality is you should because this is when the pendulum swung, in my view, all the way toward the employee by allowing him to sue for a multitude of categories of damage as opposed to simply loss of wages, which was permitted for breach of contract claims. The different categories that employees can sue under for tort claims are set forth under Sections 1.1 through and including 1.6. As referenced throughout this book, litigation dealing with employment and labor law matters is a business and it is based on economics (see Section 3.0).

Section 1.0

Why You Should Read This Book

There are two good reasons for you to read this book: 1) to avoid losing your home (because of employment litigation) and/or 2) to avoid losing your life (workplace violence).

Speaking for myself, I typically want to know the very worst that can happen in any given situation, so I can determine how much time, energy, effort, and money to dedicate to the matter. Excluding workplace violence issues, the most feared action by the employees toward their boss or supervisor is a legal claim and/or lawsuit. These can include administrative claims such as wage and hour, safety (OSHA), unemployment, workers' compensation and/or discrimination claims with administrative agencies. For those employers that have collective bargaining agreements (C.B.A.) with the unions, this can present a whole set of different problems for employers, including going through the process of grievances, work slow-downs and strikes. Additionally and of the greatest concern is that employees will retain legal counsel and pursue their claims against you in state or federal court, including claims for wrongful termination, discrimination, retaliation and related causes of action, which are substantially more expensive types of suits than are administrative claims.

As of 2005, every three seconds, 475 lawsuits are filed around the world. The United States is viewed by many as the most litigious country in the world, having had filed 10,000 discrimination lawsuits in the year 1990 and more than 20,000 discrimination lawsuits in the year 2000.

Candidly speaking, if an employee has sued you, you have already lost at least economically whether you win or lose in court. The cost just to prove you were right can be enormous. The expenses alone to hire an attorney to defend an employer or a supervisor will be in the tens if not hundreds of thousands of dollars, and the potential damages if a jury determines that you have in fact wrongfully terminated an employee is often in the hundreds of thousands of dollars or even more. Even if the employer maintains a policy of insurance, such coverage will not completely cover the supervisor or boss, as is more specifically set forth in Section 1.3 regarding punitive damages.

Employment litigation is for the most part unlike any other litigation. It is extremely emotional in that, quite frequently, people's identities are oftentimes defined by what they do for a living. When an employee relationship is severed, in many cases it is almost the same as spouses going through a divorce proceeding. This also helps to explain the high incidences of workplace violence following the termination of an employee's employment (see Section 7.0).

Caveat: After having gone through this less-than-cheerful portion of the book, you may well be considering leaving your present job and going to work as a suicide prevention counselor. It is, however, this book's premise that the personal, emotional, and financial benefits of being a boss or supervisor significantly outweigh their disadvantages. Adherence to the principles, philosophies, and practices set forth in this book will not only improve your supervisory skills, but also your people skills in general, resulting in your outlook in life improving, the air smelling better, and your becoming more attractive, rich, and happy (perhaps I exaggerated to some extent on the last comments, but reading this couldn't hurt).

> *"Before everything else,*
> *getting ready is the secret of success."*
> —Henry Ford

> *"If you have a job without aggravations,*
> *you don't have a job."*
> —Malcolm Forbes

Section 1.1: Loss-of-Wages Claim

This claim is made in virtually all employment disputes. Assume for example that your employee is thirty years of age making $30,000.00 a year and said employee claims that he was wrongfully fired or terminated by you. In this form of dispute, the employee will attempt to make a claim of future loss of wages. In making such a claim, he will argue that had he continued to work for you until the age of retirement (which would be approximately an additional 35 years until he reached at least age 65), at $30,000.00 per year or more, he would have been entitled to $900,000.00 in loss of wages. While a jury will typically not award this amount of money (hopefully because your attorney will suggest to the jury that the employee should have been able to get some type of a job between now and when he reaches age 65), the jury will still have substantial discretion. In such a situation, the jury can award anywhere between $0 and $900,000.00, and if the jury does not like the boss or supervisor, a loss-of-wages claim is a tremendous vehicle to allow a jury to significantly "hammer" the boss or supervisor.

On top of this, the employee is also entitled to receive loss of past wages, which is the amount of money he has lost from the date of the cessation of his employment to the date the jury renders a verdict, along with interest on the same.

These days, with lawsuits taking as long as two years or more before they go before a jury, the loss-of-past-wages claim alone for an employee at $30,000.00 a year would be $60,000.00 or more, plus the loss of future wages of $900,000.00.

America's first minimum wage, in 1938, was 25¢ an hour.

Section 1.2: Damages for Emotional Distress

In this category of damages, the employee's attorney may well introduce at the time of trial a psychological or a psychiatric expert to demonstrate that the employee has not only suffered loss of wages, but also significant and emotional distress. Claims of such would include evidence that the employee is suffering from weight loss or weight gain, loss of sleep, deterioration in her relationship with her family members, increased anxiety, problems with physical conditions, such as high blood pressure, chest pains, etc. In these instances, the employee's attorney will request the jury to award hundreds of thousands, if not millions of dollars. Once again, the jury has significant discretion in this category of damages and can award anywhere between zero to hundreds if not millions of dollars for the employee against the employer and/or supervisor.

Section 1.3: Punitive Damages

Punitive damages are permitted in most all employment lawsuits to make an example of the employer or supervisor, so as to make sure they never engage in such conduct again. While there are certain guidelines, there are few limits in most states on the amount that can be awarded in this category of damages.

As you may recall in the *O. J. Simpson* case, the amount of punitive damages exceeded all of the other damages put together, which is frequently the case in these types of lawsuits.

Oftentimes, juries become very emotional about the employer and/or supervisor's handling of a given situation. Juries, more frequently than not, identify with the employee more than they do with the boss or supervisor.

Keep in mind that while insurance coverage is available for various types of wrongful termination and discrimination lawsuits, not all of the areas of damages are covered. More specifically, the area of punitive damages is usually excluded. The theory behind such is that providing insurance coverage (also see Step #23) for intentional misconduct is sort of like insuring someone for engaging in criminal acts, which is against public policy and not permitted under most laws. Accordingly, if you are a supervisor working for an employer who has some insurance regarding employment matters, do not mistakenly believe that you have no personal exposure. Many employers do not have any form of insurance coverage for employment matters because the cost of such is viewed as being prohibitive, a fact of which most supervisors are unaware.

> *"It may be that your sole purpose in life*
> *is simply to serve as a warning to others."*
> —*Comedian Steve Wright*

Section 1.4: Miscellaneous Damages

If an employee has incurred out-of-pocket and/or medical and/or psychological or psychiatric expenses, the employee is permitted (if he prevails in the litigation) to recover these damages against the employer and/or supervisor. Oftentimes these can be in the tens if not hundreds of thousands of dollars, particularly in those situations where they claim that as a result of their loss of wages (see Section 1.1), they were unable to make the mortgage payments on their home and therefore had their home foreclosed upon and thereby lost significant equity in their home.

Section 1.5: Attorney's Fees

In specific employment cases (particularly those involving discrimination claims), where the employee prevails against either the boss or the supervisor, the employee is entitled to recover the value of attorney's fees that were earned by his own attorney. Oftentimes the attorney who is representing the employee doubles up and has two or more attorneys representing his client throughout the litigation at the rate of several hundred dollars per hour. Trials in these cases can last weeks, and therefore it is not unusual for the attorneys' fees to be several hundreds of thousands of dollars.

Even when bosses and supervisors prevail in the litigation, it is much more difficult, if not impossible, for them to recover their attorney's fees against the employee. This is because the bosses and/or supervisors are required to show that the employee's lawsuit was in essence frivolous. This is a different standard than is imposed upon the employee to recover his or her attorney's fees. For an employer or supervisor to prove a case to be frivolous is very difficult at the time of trial. In essence, you have to show that the employee knew at the inception of the filing of the lawsuit that the lawsuit was frivolous, which is virtually impossible to prove unless the employee admits such.

Accordingly, when bosses or supervisors are sued, they have already lost the battle economically because not only will they be responsible for their own attorney's fees, win or lose, but additionally substantial time and effort will be lost in having to defend this lawsuit for not only them but for many of their own employees who might be witnesses in the case, which is not in any manner a profitable way to do business.

The District of Columbia has one lawyer for every 19 residents.

Section 1.6: Expert Fees

In most employment cases, the boss and/or supervisor will typically have to also retain the services of a psychiatric and/or psychological expert along with an economist and frequently a human resource expert, as well as potentially a statistician. These folks charge several hundreds of dollars per hour for their time. On top of paying your own expert fees, if you lose, you will normally be required to pay the employee's expert fees. These fees again can be in the tens of thousands of dollars, if not more.

Liticaphobia – the fear of lawsuits

Section 1.7: Additional Reasons Why You Should Read this Book

The forgoing factors do not take into consideration the emotional and frequently physiological damage that you personally may suffer while this litigation lingers for up to two years or more of your life. Obviously going through this process over this duration of time, while wondering nearly every night whether or not you might lose your home, is substantially draining, not only for yourself, but also on your family members or significant others. This may have an impact on your relationship with them as well. On top of this, the stress and strain of having your deposition taken (which oftentimes can last several days), as well as going through a trial that can last for several weeks, is analogous to having an appendage severed by a dull knife.

To take an oath, ancient Romans put a hand on their testicles . . .
That's where the word "<u>testimony</u>" comes from.

Section 2.0

Thirty-One (31) Steps on How to Keep Your Home

If after having read the foregoing, I still do not have your attention, you are either in a coma or worse yet, in denial (the latter of which has helped buy several of my cars). On the other hand, like most folks when they truly understand their personal exposure in being a boss or supervisor, you are probably considering sucking out all of your automobile's carbon monoxide by putting your mouth around the exhaust pipe of your running vehicle. But wait, sit back, relax, and take a deep breath. Let us look at some less drastic options (in no particular order) that will put you in control of the situation.

"The way I see it, if you want the rainbow,
you gotta put up with the rain."
—Dolly Parton

Step #1: Always Treat Your Employees With *Respect*

In my years of working with literally hundreds upon hundreds of supervisors and managers regarding employment matters, the single greatest mistake is the failure of bosses and supervisors to treat their employees with *respect*.

Respect is not something that one can fake. If one wants to determine whether or not a person you are communicating with actually *respects* you, you typically read her face. This is done primarily because of the fact that the face has, I am advised, more than eighty nerves. Unconsciously, individuals can give all types of signs showing they really do not *respect* the person with whom they are communicating. This can be through rolling of the eyes, certain facial glitches, as well as body language, etc.

Once any supervisor or boss has communicated to an employee any non-verbal signs of disrespect, it will be very difficult for that supervisor or manager to ever gain that person's *respect* again. IF SOMEONE DOES NOT *RESPECT* YOU, MOST LIKELY YOU WILL NOT *RESPECT* HIM.

Any time bosses or supervisors fail to show *respect* toward the persons with whom they are working, it is a clear showing that these managers are lacking in supervisory skills and is a strong indication that they will be having problems with the persons with whom they are working.

Even if you have to fire someone, you can still treat her with dignity and respect. Remember, treating persons with *respect* shows that you are in control. Treating even difficult employees with *respect* in the short term helps you in the long term. Not only does it substantially decrease the likelihood that you will be sued personally, but further, building such a reputation will help you personally in the long term in both your personal and professional life. Your reputation defines who you are in the employment world.

> *"The best index to a person's character is*
> *how he treats people who can't do him any good,*
> *and how he treats people who can't fight back."*
> *—Abigail Van Buren*

> *An example of not treating individuals with respect –*
> *"I would like to take you seriously,*
> *but to do so would affront your intelligence."*
> *—William F. Buckley*

> *"The time is always right to do what is right."*
> *—Dr. Martin Luther King, Jr.*

"Diplomacy: The art of saying 'nice doggy'
until you can find a rock."
—*Mark Twain*

Step #2: Remember the "Blue-Haired-Lady Doctrine"

Because of the nature of our legal system, a significant portion of most jury panels is made up of senior citizens. No matter how great a boss or supervisor's attorney might be or how great you perceive the facts to be in your favor, the reality is that most likely the person having a significant impact on whether or not you prevail at the time of trial will rest with one or more senior citizens (a.k.a., a "Blue-Haired Lady"). These individuals may well have been in their thirties or forties when your attorney was born and really do not care about the significance or manner of presentation of your legal argument, cases, and statutes. Rather, when they get into the jury room, they often decide a case on what they perceive to be fair and/or just.

It is because of this common-sense approach (with the possible exception of the O. J. Simpson case), that our jury system has no equal. Accordingly, a good rule to keep in mind is to ask yourself whether or not a "Blue-Haired Lady" (perhaps it is your mother or grandmother—unless they were convicted felons) would agree with whatever approach you have taken in a given employment situation. Chances are, if your own mother or grandmother would perceive your conduct to be appropriate, so most likely would a jury. Keep in mind, however, that the opposite is true as well. Stated another way, simply use common sense. However, as Voltaire once stated: "Common sense is not too common." Accordingly, using this doctrine may come in handy.

"Common sense often makes good law."
—*William O. Douglas,*
United States Supreme Court Justice (1939-1975)

Step #3: Have Well-Prepared Employment Applications

Let's face it, when people come to apply for employment they will typically sign most anything the employer puts before them. Accordingly this is one of those rare opportunities where a boss or supervisor has an opportunity to take some affirmative action to immediately assert control and reduce liability.

All too often, people believe that employment applications are simply form documents created by an anal computer that was programmed to waste people's time. Quite to the contrary, if properly drafted, the application can be a better friend to you than a postal supervisor's bulletproof vest. Frequently, many employers do not even use application forms or when they do, they use the standardized versions that are obtained at the local stationery store. It is suggested that if you're going to use standardized forms, use those that have been approved by employer-oriented groups or associations. In the alternative, have a qualified attorney prepare one for you. The contents of these applications should include the following:

(A) General background information: name, telephone number, address, e-mail, veteran status, social security number (all to be guarded as confidential).

(B) The name, address and telephone number of at least four non-family/friend references.

(C) Questions requesting information about all prior places of employment, as well as the duration of said employment and the reasons for the cessation of said employment.

(D) Questions as to whether or not the applicant has committed a felony within the last seven years. Do not ask for details of the felony unless you want to establish a policy that you may under some circumstances (such as non-violence or non-drug related offenses) allow some felons to work for you.

(E) Immediately above where the employee will place his signature, there should be a couple paragraphs of rather self-serving language for the employer establishing the fact that the applicant understands that he will be an "at will" employee, as well as defining that term (see Step 14). Additionally, if your company is going to have any type of drug testing, it is advisable also to include that language in this portion of the application. Furthermore, include language confirming if there is any false information provided in the application by the applicant that such may result in cessation of the applicant's employment any time during the employee's employment. Furthermore, it is helpful to include in this portion of the application that if any dispute arises between the employee and the employer, such will be resolved by way of binding arbitration (see Step #13). Additionally, you might want to include language that specifies that if the applicant is agreeable, that once he becomes an employee that his final paycheck may be mailed to him. The legality of any of the foregoing may vary from jurisdiction to jurisdiction, and therefore it is always advisable to consult for an hour or two with a qualified attorney in this area.

(F) Make sure the application does not include any questions relating to the applicant's sex, age (unless it is confirming that the individual is over the age of eighteen), marital status, religion, medical history, sexual orientation, pregnancy, disability, or any other protected classifications. Many applications improperly inquire as to whether or not the applicant has a disability, and if so, what accommodation he is seeking for said disability. Any questions regarding disability and/or accommodations should not be asked until the applicant has conditionally been offered a job. To do otherwise may be considered a violation of the applicant's right of privacy and also quite possibly be construed as discriminatory. After the conditional offer has been made, then it is permissible to go into these areas to determine whether or not the accommodation that is necessary for the applicant to perform the normal job duties and responsibilities is in fact reasonable. Again, this area of determination should involve the advice of legal counsel.

(G) In the law in some jurisdictions, there is the "After Acquired Evidence Doctrine." This doctrine provides that if an employee lied on her application when you hired her, and you relied on such, you have several benefits. Not only can you fire her for such, but also if she later sues you (even for some unrelated discrimination claim), you can introduce her application (even years after she prepared such) to attack not only her credibility, but also to eliminate her claims for certain types of damages. You cannot use this, however, if she just left a blank on the application, so make sure all your applicants fill out the entire application form completely.

Step #4: Screen and Interview Properly

Because of the importance and complexity of this issue, it is set forth in its own separate section, at section 4.0 et seq.

Step #5: Conduct Exit Interviews

A simplified exit interview form is a one-page document that can be prepared by the boss or supervisor, which indicates at the top of the page, the letterhead of the boss followed thereafter by the name of the employee, the date of the document, and then the general heading "Comments." At the bottom of the page is a place for the signature of the employee. The employer hopefully has a personnel manual, which mandates that all terminating (whether it be voluntary or involuntary) employees complete this form. If an employee refuses to comply with this policy, you may ask what are you then going to do. Firing an employee twice is not particularly helpful. However, in most instances employees will fill out the form either because it is a written policy or they are more than happy to tell you what they think of you at such a time, so take advantage of this opportunity. The benefits of having an exit interview form filled out by the employee include the following:

(A) Generally, whatever the employee puts down on the exit interview form is deemed a legal admission. Oftentimes it is not until after the former employee meets with his attorney that the employee determines that he was somehow discriminated against. In such cases, the employee does not usually put anything down about discrimination in the exit interview form. Consequently, when he is asked on the witness stand about how two years previously at the time of his termination when he filled out the exit interview form (when his memory was much better than it is today), that he said nothing about discrimination; however, now after spending two years with his attorney, he is now claiming discrimination; and therefore, should the jury believe him then or now?

(B) Exit interview forms also allow employees to vent their hostilities. Frequently litigation occurs because employees feel that they were ignored or not *respected*. Therefore, allowing them to vent oftentimes provides an escape vehicle for their emotions and also can be helpful in avoiding workplace violence situations. For the same reasons, an anonymous employee suggestion box is also advisable for your business.

(C) Finally, the employee may well provide information to the employer in an exit interview form that is helpful to either the boss or supervisor. You should at all times be open to receive constructive feedback of any kind from all employees. If you are not, it is highly unlikely that your employees will be receptive regarding your constructive criticism.

> *Everyone has a photographic memory;*
> *some just don't have film.*
> *—Anonymous*

Step #6: Buy Time

Whenever reasonably possible, avoid making an important decision on the spot. Rather, always give yourself an opportunity to carefully consider the situation, and if necessary, so as to allow you to consult with others. Making decisions on the spot typically works to the advantage of the employee and to the disadvantage of the boss or supervisor. Accordingly, the next time an employee presents a serious or complicated issue to you, rather than giving an immediate response (which many bosses and supervisors frequently do to demonstrate how smart they are), simply tell the employee, "I WILL GET BACK TO YOU." Make sure, however, that you do in fact get back to her within a reasonable time frame.

"Time cools, time clarifies; no mood can be maintained quite unaltered through the course of hours."
—Mark Twain

"By swallowing evil words unsaid,
no one has ever harmed his stomach."
—Winston Churchill

Step #7: Offer Resignation Versus Firing

Rarely, if at all, does an attorney ever tell a client that there is one general rule in employment that should always apply. This, however, is one of those rare situations. No matter what the circumstances or situation (even if the employee was caught red-handed making live copies of the boss' drunk daughter's posterior on the company's copy machine), the employee should still be offered the opportunity to resign instead of being fired.

A prime reason for this approach is that most employees' attorneys are known to reject what are referred to as constructive discharge lawsuits. These are cases where the employee is forced to quit rather than voluntarily quitting him or herself. The primary goal typically in the employer/employment relationship is to have a mutually beneficial relationship. Remember, if you get to the point where the employment relationship is no longer beneficial to you, your primary goal at this stage should be either to make it beneficial or to get out of the relationship and to avoid litigation. In avoiding litigation, make sure that the factual pattern is as unattractive as is reasonably possible to an employee's potential attorney. Most jurors do not get as upset about an employer forcing an employee to quit, as opposed to actually firing him. For that reason, these cases are less attractive to employees' attorneys.

Keep in mind however, that this approach can sometimes backfire when it is abundantly clear that the boss or supervisor crossed the line in putting pressure on the employee to quit. An example of such occurred several years ago wherein the boss literally went up to the employee on several consecutive days and slapped him, resulting in the employee finally quitting. This is not going to be received particularly well by a "Blue-Haired Lady."

As a general rule, however, an employer offering an employee the opportunity to resign can be mutually beneficial. This allows the employee to have some level of dignity if she so chooses. Furthermore, this at least gives the employee a choice, and some degree of control and therefore dignity and *respect*. Frequently, employees will elect this option because it looks better on their resumes than does a firing. From an employer's standpoint, there is really no down side to allowing an employee to resign.

Over the years several managers and supervisors have indicated that they do not want to allow an employee the privilege to resign. This is because it appears to them that there is some type of ratification of the employee's conduct by allowing an employee to resign. Respectfully, this is a very narrow and shortsighted approach. The primary method to avoid litigation is making sure that the fact pattern is as unattractive as is reasonably possible to an employee's potential attorney.

When an employer gets to the ultimate sanction of terminating the employment relationship, the goal should be to simply get the employee out of the door as cheaply, reasonably, and professionally as is possible while at the same time minimizing the risk of litigation. Allowing an employee to resign accomplishes all of these tasks. The failure to consider such has resulted in many bosses and supervisors moving from their homes into rental units.

For the most part employees will not accept this option because of their perception that such will eliminate their chances for receiving unemployment. However, even if you get one out of ten, you as a boss or supervisor are still way ahead of the game. Furthermore, in most jurisdictions, qualifying for unemployment is premised upon why the employees quit or were fired, not on whether or not they quit or were fired.

> *FIRED — There was a term used back first in 1871 referred to as "fired out." This meant to throw out or eject someone from a place or location. A few years later, the term "out" was dropped and the phrase was limited to mean "dismissal of an employee." It appears according to the experts, that both terms "fired" and "fired out" made references to a gun being fired.*

Step #8: Consider Other Options Besides Firing

Just like the old Paul Simon song, "There must be fifty ways to leave your lover," there must be the same or more methods to have an employee get her act together besides the ultimate sanction of firing. As a general rule, bosses and supervisors (like everyone else) want to avoid confrontation. It is for this reason that frequently bosses and supervisors, rather than positively and constructively trying to educate their employees, simply elect to terminate their employment. This approach is not only dangerous litigation wise, it is also a strong indicator of how poor a job the supervisor is actually doing.

> *Accordingly, just because you might have the power to fire someone, consider other options as was stated by Abraham Lincoln: "Nearly all men can stand adversity, but if you want to test a man's character, give him power."*

All too frequently supervisors complain: "But if we only had competent employees, we could do a much better job." In the words of Homer Simpson: "D'oh!" The reality is that for the most part, how poor an employee performs is more a reflection of poor supervision and lack of training as opposed to an indicator of an employee's ability. Anyone can take a good employee and do a good job; however, it takes a good supervisor to direct an inexperienced employee to do a good job. Often that is what the job requires. If all employees were outstanding and didn't need supervision, we wouldn't need supervisors and managers. The best bosses and supervisors are those who are respectful, creative, constructive, and positive in working *with* their employees, as well as those who like what they are doing.

When you fire an employee, you have admitted that you have made at least two mistakes. One is that you let the person get into the door to begin with, and the second is that you were unable to train the individual to make her productive. In either case, the reality is that when you replace an employee for performance reasons you will spend two to six months on average training his or her replacement.

Further, firing employees creates unnecessary insecurity in the work force and results in decreased morale. Options available besides firing include providing verbal reprimands, written reprimands, demotion, suspension without pay, reduction in pay, reduction in benefits, reduction in hours for hourly employees, and a multitude of other alternatives.

It is advisable whenever possible to improve performance by positive reinforcement such as complimenting their work (particularly in the presence of their colleagues), providing parking spaces or plaques for employees of the month, or almost any form of positive acknowledgment. Most all of the foregoing can be done without any significant cost. There are of course the monetary reinforcements, which include promotions, raises, and bonuses.

"You know what makes leadership?
It is the ability to get men to do what
they don't want to do, and like it."
—President Harry Truman

Other options besides firing include transfers. Frequently, a transfer, which may well in reality be a demotion, will most likely not result in litigation where the employee continues to receive the same compensation as what he was receiving in his prior job. These are not moneymakers for employees' attorneys, and they often will not take such cases.

Keep in mind that litigation is primarily based upon economics as opposed to right and wrong. Simply stated, an employees' attorney will not take a lawsuit unless she believes that she can convince a "Blue-Haired Lady" that her client was harmed. Most "Blue-Haired Ladies" do not get particularly emotional about transfers with the same or similar pay as to what the employee was making before the transfer. However, transfers that are made for clearly inappropriate or discriminatory reasons, such as the employee's sex, age, race, marital status, religion etc., will oftentimes be pursued by employees' attorneys.

"I'm old? When you were young, the Dead Sea was only sick!"
—Milton Berle

"She was so old, when she went to school
they didn't have history."
—Comedian Rodney Dangerfield

Step #9: Consider Severance Pay

Contrary to popular belief, this does not refer to severing various parts of the body of the problem employee. Rather, providing severance pay is oftentimes an unknown or forgotten option. In utilizing this approach, the employee is terminated and at the same time receives some additional compensation so as to allow the employee to move on with his life. Severance pay is oftentimes based on two weeks to three months of the employee's regular pay (however, there is no legal minimum or maximum limit). The employee is required to complete a release agreement waiving any and all claims and rights regarding litigation against the employer, and in some instances waiving the right to reemployment.

Remember, if you fire an employee and she signs a release and gets severance pay, she still has the right to come back and reapply to you for employment; and if you refuse to hire her, she can claim that is retaliation and sue you again for six- or seven-digit numbers, claiming that you did not rehire her because of her former complaints.

Severance pay can be provided without the employee being required to execute a release agreement. Some employers trying to be nice to the terminated employee have done this. However, in most instances where the employee is inclined to sue, this gesture by the employer holds little weight. From a legal standpoint, this simply makes no sense. At a minimum the employer should write on the reverse side of the severance pay check (typically above where the employee's endorsement will be written), language such as "Full and final settlement of any and all claims of any kind." Such language may not in all cases be enforceable, as would a detailed written release agreement; however, it is better than no agreement at all.

It is preferable to have a written release agreement prepared by a qualified attorney. There have been many examples when the agreement was not carefully drafted and where the employee was still entitled to receive the severance pay and at the same time still be able to sue, such as in the case of age-discrimination claims.

The amount of the severance pay may vary dramatically depending upon the factual situation involved. Factors to consider regarding severance pay include the employee's tenure, the boss and supervisor's potential liability, the likelihood of litigation, as well as concerns as to what type of precedent the boss or supervisor is setting by making such payments.

In the majority of terminations of employment, the boss or supervisor will not want to pay out severance in that there is little or no threat and/or little or no exposure of liability. In those situations where there is the likelihood of liability, oftentimes paying severance pay is much better than incurring tens of thousands of dollars in attorneys' fees, and potentially hundreds of thousands of dollars from an adverse jury verdict.

The bottom line: if you think that the termination of a particular employee may attract a plaintiff's attorney, you should consider as an option severance pay. Always consult an attorney on this issue before taking what should normally be this fairly rare action.

Top three "problem" employees,
according to the Wall Street Journal:
#1 "The Nonstop Talker"
#2 "The Screamer"
#3 "The Practical Joker"

Step #10: Maintain Written Policies

Personnel handbooks (when followed) are a tremendous device to assist employers in avoiding liability. Just like anything else, however, they should not be drafted in the extreme. Over the years, I have reviewed employee manuals ranging in size from two pages to several hundred pages in length. Ironically, the latter can be just as dangerous as the former. Having a lengthy personnel handbook covering every theoretical problem that might arise often results in less flexibility for the employer. Further they are often ignored by bosses, supervisors, and employees simply because they are too long.

"Any fool can make something complex;
it takes a genius to make something simple."
—Pete Seeger

On the other hand, having a two-page policy that basically tells employees that they are to do what they are told is not particularly productive, nor serves any real benefit to either the employer or the employee. A properly drafted handbook provides an opportunity to not only sell (in a very positive manner) the employer to the employee, but it also serves as a cheap and efficient manner of educating the employees of what is expected of them. This approach is far better than repeatedly going through the time-consuming process of doing such verbally, which oftentimes results in miscommunication.

The quality of personnel handbooks varies as much as does the quality of employees. Be very careful about participating in the common practice of plagiarizing other companies' policy handbooks. The lack or inclusion of one or two words in a seventy-page manual can have a significant impact upon the employer, all of which could have been avoided by spending a few hours with a qualified attorney. If litigation does occur, personnel handbooks can provide significant defenses to the boss/supervisor; therefore make sure they are properly drafted.

It is also advisable to have the handbooks/manuals drafted in a somewhat positive form as opposed to simply laying out rules and regulations. These can come off as very impersonal and cold to the new employee. At the very inception of the handbook, the employer will want to establish in the introduction the various attributes of the employer. This is where you make it clear that you have high expectations on quality as well as the fact that you view your employees as your primary asset.

Many personnel handbooks start off with a listing of all the reasons that an employee can be fired. This is not going to give a new employee a warm and fuzzy feeling about working for your business. On average, most personnel handbooks can be drafted for about five to ten hours of attorney time, which is typically a good investment for the employer in the long run. Some policies and laws are mandated to be posted by the employer by state, federal, and foreign laws regarding particular areas, such as wage and hour requirements, rights regarding discrimination, overtime, rights to vote during working days, sexual harassment, etc. The personnel handbook is the ideal vehicle for the posting and publication of such information. Providing employee handbooks to employees before problems arise often prevents such problems.

"Take time to repair the roof when the sun is shining."
—John F. Kennedy

Step #11: Provide Written Evaluations

A good employment practice, as well as a key defense to avoiding liability, is to provide to employees (typically on an annual basis) written evaluations regarding their performance. These evaluations need to be accurate as well as constructive. In this manner, bosses and supervisors can provide feedback to employees relating to their performance. Additionally, this creates a paper trail so as to make it clear to both the employee and, if necessary, a jury at a later date, that the problems (and your efforts to resolve them) have been ongoing.

The only thing worse than no evaluation is the frequently followed practice of providing positive evaluations to lousy employees. Purportedly, this is done to motivate them to do a better job. Such false evaluations never motivate employees to do a better job. Rather they typically serve as a catalyst for lousy employees to do even worse, because they perceive that their low level of performance is acceptable. It's rather embarrassing a year down the road to confront an employee about a history of poor performance (or to try and claim in front of a jury that an employee has been having substantial problems for a lengthy period of time) only to look back in the employee's personnel file and find an evaluation form that ranks the person second only to God.

On the other hand, I have heard experts suggest that nothing should be put into an employee's personnel file except negative remarks and comments. Respectfully this is not only unfair to the employee, but it also creates a rift between the employee and his supervisor. Finally, this carries little credibility with "Blue-Haired Ladies" on jury panels. It is more likely that they will view such negativism more as a supervisorial problem, as opposed to an employee problem. An evaluation or even memorandums to an employee's personnel file that reflects both positive and negative aspects of an employee's performance demonstrates to the employee, as well as everyone else, that the supervisor is objective and credible. You can always find something positive to put on an evaluation form, even if it is only that the employee is breathing properly.

When doing the evaluation, don't simply hand the form to the employee. Verbally discuss with the employee your evaluation and explain your rationale (both good and bad) in a constructive, diplomatic manner, so as to make it clear to the employee that you *respect* and care about him. This is not something that you can fake.

Employees, just like most other persons, are experts on a twenty-four hour, seven-day basis in judging others and in particular, judging how others perceive and *respect* them. A sneer, smirk, frown, etc., while frequently being done in an inadvertent manner, conveys to the recipient how you really feel about her. Accordingly, whenever, you are doing an evaluation, always start by pointing out some positive aspects to the employee about herself. Otherwise, if you are only critical without conveying that you have *respect* and genuinely care about the person to whom you are talking, she will care very little, if at all, about what you have to say. This suggestion is helpful not only in the employer/employee relationship, but in any personal relationship.

> *While it is true that a lot of employees complain about*
> *the issue of pay, surveys show that fifty-three percent*
> *of Americans think that they are paid the proper amount.*

Step #12: Invest in Training and Education

A substantial portion of disharmony involving employees, as well as litigation, could be avoided simply by providing more training to supervisors, in particular as to how to deal with people, as well as employment practices, laws, and procedures. Employers oftentimes ignore such training because the financial return on such an investment is not immediately ascertainable. Typically, the best employers are those that have been through the litigation process in one degree or another and understand that it is better to invest minimal amounts in training and education up front, versus significant amounts later in retraining replacements and/or retaining attorneys.

For the most part, bosses and supervisors' training is either by word of mouth and/or on-the-job training, which is sometimes combined with a brief orientation process. This procedure is about as effective as bringing in a union to increase your employee's productivity levels. Effective options for training and education (besides reading this outstanding book) include a formalized orientation program, seminars, a mentoring program (wherein one employee is designated as a type of big brother or sister to another employee), other books, videos, etc. The amount of training and education will of course vary with the various jobs involved.

The weakest link typically in the employment chain, however, has been mid-management. These are usually individuals who have been rapidly transferred to supervisory positions with little or no training and make big mistakes that are very costly for the employer, and then ask for a raise.

As it relates to education and training, as well as obtaining advice from "consultants" on human resource matters, BE VERY CAREFUL. These days there is a glut of so-called human resource consultants who frequently create more problems than they cure. There is little or no regulation or licensing in this area, except for attorneys who are too expensive for the day-to-day problems the boss or supervisor encounters. Accordingly, most small companies hire employees to serve several functions including human resources, and then send these employees out for training. Larger companies will want skilled professionals with either college degrees in human resources, or years of experience, or both. Be leery of the so-called "Human Resource Consultants" without first checking out their credentials, references, and experience in litigation.

> *"It is noble to teach oneself,*
> *but still nobler to teach others –*
> *and less trouble."*
> *—Mark Twain*

Step #13: Have an Arbitration Provision

This is a rapidly evolving theory of law developing throughout the employment world. Many jurisdictions provide that employees and employers can voluntarily agree to have any and all disputes existing between them resolved by way of binding arbitration, as opposed to being resolved by way of a jury trial. This approach is significantly beneficial to a boss or supervisor, in that juries are frequently unpredictable and typically viewed more as being employee-oriented. Therefore, it makes sense for bosses and supervisors, whenever reasonably possible, to have all disputes with employees be resolved by way of binding arbitration. This is typically done with a retired judge or attorney who is experienced in employment matters. All too frequently in employment disputes, the juries view the employee as David and view the employer as Goliath, a mindset that has frequently resulted in runaway jury verdicts.

The problem with arbitrations is that oftentimes what an employer considers to be a voluntary agreement by the employee is not considered such by the courts, nor usually the employee. Most often this occurs where the employee is making a claim of discrimination in one of the protected categories, including sex, age, race, marital status, religion, sexual orientation, pregnancy, etc.

As a result, there have been a multitude of cases setting forth specific factors with which an employer has to comply in order to successfully enforce a binding arbitration agreement in a personnel handbook. In general, the provision in the personnel handbook has to be clearly understood by the employee, and in essence (with the exception of substituting a retired judge for the jury), cannot be in any manner one-sided or eliminate any other rights that an employee would have if he had gone through a regular jury trial.

In addition, the employer cannot unfairly burden the employee with the cost of such a process and further cannot force the employee to agree to such, in discrimination disputes in particular. Because of all these parameters, the reality is that any knowledgeable employee would be foolish to enter into such an arrangement. However, the benefits to some employees include the fact that it is much more expedient, arguably less stressful and cheaper, which is why in some instances some employees have voluntarily agreed to arbitrations.

In order to make sure that you have an enforceable binding arbitration provision in your personnel handbook, competent legal counsel should be consulted.

"They added up all the people in this country who consider themselves a minority, and it added up to more than the population of the country."
—Bill Maher, TV political talk show host

Step #14: Maintain the "At Will" Doctrine (see Section 8.2)

Essentially there are two forms of employment, one being "at will" and the other being that you can only terminate an employee for "good cause." It is typically beneficial for a boss and supervisor to assert the former, inasmuch as the burden and the justification required to justify firing an employee to a jury is much less if the employee is considered to be "at will." This is why typically you will find "at will" language not only in the employment applications (if properly drafted) but also in the personnel handbook and various other policies and procedures that the employer might have.

Since 1877 starting in California, the law recognized that an employer may terminate an employee's employment with or without cause and with or without notice. This is simply referred to as "at will" employment. While this means that you may terminate an employee with or without cause or with or without notice, it does not mean that you can terminate/discipline an employee for an improper cause, such as because they belong to any of the protected categories including sex, race, age, marital status, religion, etc., nor for unlawful purposes, such as whistle blowing, voting contrary to the way that you want them to vote, etc. The law generally presumes that employees are "at will" and therefore, it's not necessary for you to assert such. However, it is easy to waive this presumption.

Unfortunately, this doctrine can be waived if the boss or supervisor engages in conduct that leads the employee to personally believe that she can only be terminated for good cause. Examples of such conduct include a boss or supervisor telling an employee: "You have a job here for life" or "You can continue working here until you retire or die," etc. More likely examples are when a boss or supervisor puts an employee on "probation." Technically "at will" employees are always on probation, and therefore if you tell an employee he is on probation, he assumes that once he gets off the probation, he can only be terminated for a good cause. That is why most employers no longer have a probationary period at the beginning of an employee's employment. Rather, they now refer to such as an introductory period. Words are extremely important in employment litigation.

In summary, it's important for bosses and supervisors to understand this doctrine, not so they can assert such, but more importantly so they make sure they do not waive it by making any type of representations regarding duration of employment which is contrary to "at will" employment.

"It is better to offer no excuse than a bad one."
—George Washington

Step #15: Be Aware of the Trickle-Down Theory

While there continue to be debates on whether or not the trickle-down theory of economics works, it is clear that it applies in the employment world. More specifically, the boss and supervisor are indeed role models for their employee's performance, behavior, attitude, and morale. For example, assume that the president of a company is having a bad-hair day and she comes in and yells at the Senior Vice President. The Senior Vice President then out of anger and frustration unjustifiably yells at the Junior Vice President. The Junior Vice President in turn does the same thing to the General Manager and so on and so on until finally the Senior File Clerk yells at the Junior File Clerk, resulting in the Junior File Clerk going home and kicking his dog.

Keep in mind that traditionally and usually justifiably both the credit and the blame for the day-to-day relations between management and staff starts at the top. Always remember that the company works as a team and make sure that all staff treats one another with *respect*. Furthermore, right, wrong, or indifferent, it's very important for bosses and supervisors to maintain not only a positive, but also a "go get 'em" attitude.

> *"Example is not the main thing in influencing others.*
> *It is the only thing."*
> *—Dr. Albert Schweitzer*

> *"I hear and I forget. I see and I remember.*
> *I do and I understand."*
> *—Confucius*

Step #16: Avoid Negativism

> *"Whining is anger coming out of a small hole."*
> *—Al Franken, quoted in the Denver Post*

Everyone has a bad-hair day. The goal is to avoid either yourself or your employees having bad-hair weeks or perhaps even months. Oftentimes, bosses and supervisors overreact to minor problems resulting in them becoming disasters. There is a substantial difference between negativism and constructive criticism. The former typically involves complaints about obvious problems, without solutions. Constructive criticism not only points out deficiencies but also has solutions for those problems, which is what you want to get from your employees. Make it clear, even in your employee handbook, that you expect the latter and have no time for the former.

"Cynicism: The intellectual cripple's substitute for intelligence."
—*Russell Lynes*

"Any fool can criticize, and many of them do."
—*Cyril Garbett*

"Any fool can criticize, condemn, and complain –
and most fools do."
—*Benjamin Franklin*

Additionally (in dealing with employees), it's important for bosses and supervisors to remember that you can always be an S.O.B. at any time. So you really have nothing to lose by at least starting off with a positive approach. In dealing with employee problems, I recall the old adage my father used to tell me which was: "The only person that doesn't make a mistake is the one who doesn't do a damn thing." Basically, most companies want employees who are not only self-starters but also learn from their mistakes. This includes supervisors as well. Bosses and supervisors need to create an environment where it is understood that while employees should certainly avoid mistakes, it's not constructive for them to wallow in self-pity, so long as the employee has learned from his or her mistakes and the employer did not have to file bankruptcy.

Speak when you are angry and you'll make
the best speech you'll ever regret.
—*Lawrence J. Peter*

"The best way to cheer yourself up: cheer everybody else up."
—*Mark Twain*

"The greater part of our happiness or misery depends on our
dispositions and not our circumstances."
—*Martha Washington*

Step #17: Avoid the Rumor Mill

Rumors can be a serious problem in the workplace. Oftentimes, rumors spread faster than office emails and can be extremely damaging, as well as lead to workplace violence when carried out to the extreme.

Several years ago, an employment law attorney represented a company who had two groups of secretaries who were spreading vicious rumors about one another. It got to be a competition to see who could harm which group the most, resulting in one of the participants placing on another one of the separate groups' windshield a photograph of that individual's husband and another female in a rather compromising position. As you might imagine, such does not exactly build up employee morale.

Rumors frequently result in good employees leaving, as well as causing decreased productivity and an overall negative working atmosphere. In order to reduce such conduct, it is helpful to make it clear that persons who engage in this type of conduct typically have little or no life. Further that their spreading of such rumors is the only manner in which their otherwise insignificant existence apparently creates some degree of purpose, which of course is a very sad commentary. (It's actually helpful to put an anti-rumor policy in your personnel handbook setting forth your views on rumors, along the foregoing lines.)

> **GOSSIP**: *when you hear something you like*
> *about someone you don't.*
> —*Earl Wilson*

Step #18: Maintain a Reasonable Working Environment

The environment in the workplace itself can mean more than all the bonuses and raises that can be accumulated. More specifically, employees are like anyone else in that they, like you, want to go to a place not only where they are *respected*, but a place where each day they get up and hopefully look forward to coming to work. This atmosphere at work can consist not only in the manner in which the people treat one another, but also the physical environment as well.

Oftentimes the most common complaints that arise in the work environment are between males and females fighting over the thermostat in an office. The females are frequently freezing wherein the males are dying of heat exhaustion, and accordingly many thermostats are located in an area and subject only to being adjusted by an office manager. Keep in mind the sensitivities of the persons who are working in the office and try to work a reasonable compromise for all persons concerned.

Studies have indicated that music coming into the workplace can increase productivity; however, that is obviously dependent upon what type of music is piped into an office space. As a result, most bosses and supervisors select music that is hated the least or viewed as boring by everyone, which frequently results in many Barry Manilow songs being played.

There are additional studies showing that simply allowing office personnel to walk in their stocking feet so as to make their workplace more comfortable increases productivity for a short period of time, but then returns back to the normal production levels. Put another way, any time employers treat their employees as if they are other than numbers and view them as more important than the job that they are performing, the results are an increase in production, whether it be white-collar or blue-collar workers.

"He is well paid that is well satisfied."
—Shakespeare

Not to be confused with employees,
but studies show that cows give more milk
when they listen to music.

Scientific studies show that the smell of peppermint
improves the concentration of office workers.

Another factor to keep in mind is the teaming up of workers. An example I have given over the years is that of my wife and myself. We both have been quite successful in our respective professions, she as an elementary school principal and myself as an attorney; however, we would not make a good team working together. My wife has always been the type of person to be extremely well organized, color coding, indexing and alphabetizing nearly everything she touches. I, on the other hand, tend not to be so organized; and as a result, my wife and others have commented on more than one occasion about the possibility that perhaps small children have been lost in the clutter on my desk. On the other hand, I look at my wife as the type of person to clean lint out of a flea's navel, and consequently we would not be a good working team. Keep that in mind when determining which of your employees will work with one another.

On a separate note, as it relates to the working environment, be sensitive to circumstances in the work environment that can cause illness or allergies or other general discomfort. It is not unusual for employers to have specific written policies in their handbooks that prohibit employees from utilizing colognes or perfumes that might impact or affect other employees. In addition, personal hygiene can be a real problem in the workplace, and therefore again it is most important to have existing employee policies and a written employee handbook or manual requiring employees to exercise reasonable hygiene.

On top of this, it is of course important to maintain a clean working atmosphere in that I have personally defended one employer on a seven-digit claim wherein a multitude of employees got together and asserted that mold had developed in the air conditioning system of the place of employment, causing fatigue and other side effects. Therefore make sure your work environment is in compliance with all state, federal, and foreign laws as well as being a reasonable habitat that would be acceptable to a "Blue-Haired Lady." Recent studies have shown that employees' desks (because of eating at the desk as well as female makeup, etc.) have more bacteria than the average bathroom. Female's desks have been shown to have more bacteria than males, apparently because of makeup and more eating at their desks.

Bottom line: make sure that your place of employment is kept clean and reasonable, if not only just to avoid employees becoming ill and having unnecessary downtime.

Surveys have shown that one percent of businesses located in the United States actually allow their employees to take naps during their hours of work.

There have been studies conducted showing that a view of forestry can expedite patients' recovery time in hospitals as well as increase the productivity of employees and reduce their stress levels in the workplace.

Step #19: Avoid Favoritism

The realities are that people typically favor individuals for a variety of reasons. Problems occur in the workplace when favoritism is not work-related. Initially, avoid such conduct and prevent such from happening in the workplace because it can become terribly destructive.

Another problem that arises is the situation where the supervisor or boss shows her favoritism toward an employee who is doing a good job by simply giving that individual more duties and responsibilities without any real incentives. Keep in mind there are a multitude of methods by which to reward employees for good performance including providing compliments (particularly in the presence of their colleagues), performance letters to their personnel files, individualized parking spaces, any recognition program pointing out outstanding performance, additional benefits, additional vacation time, gift certificates, positive written evaluations, as well as of course promotions and raises. It is not always necessary to provide financial awards, but rather simply some recognition for a job well done.

Problems occur in the workplace when favoritism is not premised on good work performance, but rather on non-work-related conduct, such as social relationships, blood relatives, etc. Even when justified in the work atmosphere, favoritism is unbecoming of a boss or supervisor in that, as referenced previously, bosses and supervisors should not become friends with or date any of the individuals whom they supervise. While it makes sense to trust the better-qualified individual with the more important responsibilities, keep in mind that you do not want to burn out your good employees by rewarding them with harder work, especially if it's for the same pay that is being received by the poorer employees. Make sure you always maintain incentives to motivate the good employees to do a better job. This is an acceptable method of favoritism.

> *"You want a friend in Washington, get a dog."*
> *—President Harry Truman*

Step #20: Be Aware of the Black, Gray, and Red Zones

There are really three zones within which a boss and supervisor can operate. The first zone is referred to as the "black zone," which is typically the safe zone of operations. The next zone is the "gray zone" where the rules, laws, and regulations are not as clear. The final zone is the "red zone" where it is abundantly clear that you've crossed the line. In the red zone, any reasonably objective person could (i.e., failure to obtain workers' compensation insurance or pay overtime, for example) look at the circumstances and realize that someone knowingly crossed the line, but apparently was willing to take the risk in doing such.

These zones can apply to all aspects of work, as well as life. If it weren't for bosses and supervisors crossing the gray and red zones, employment attorneys would not be in business. The zone that's typically of most concern is the gray zone in that this is the area wherein rationalization frequently takes over, and the boss and/or supervisor oftentimes get into this zone without actually knowing that they're there. As I have always heard, the biggest problems are not the ones that you're aware of, but rather the ones that hit you on your blind side.

An illustration of these zones would be as follows:

(A) Black zone – You come to work and greet your subordinates by wishing them a good morning. Clearly this is in the black zone in that no one would reasonably question your actions in this regard.

(B) Gray zone – Now you come into work in the morning; however, this time not only do you wish your subordinate a good morning, but also you place your hand on her body. If you place a hand on her back, most likely it's not a problem; however if you massage her back, there could be a problem.

(C) Red zone – In this case, you come into work in the morning and pat the subordinate on her bottom. In this instance, you clearly crossed into the danger or red zone, and anyone objectively looking at what you have done would know that you're probably a fan of magazines with naked iguanas.

Most litigation arises from bosses and supervisors engaging in acts that cross into the gray to the red zone. For many bosses and supervisors, it is a justified business risk to go into the gray zone, and this is quite common in that frequently business involves risk-taking. However, it is always important to make sure you know precisely what those risks are.

"It takes twenty years to build a reputation and five minutes to ruin it. If you think about that, you'll do things differently."
—Warren Buffet

Step #21: Use "Advice of Counsel" Defense

Another defense available to employers regarding these claims is "Advice of counsel." The courts have decided that if it can be proven by the boss or supervisor that he disclosed all material facts to his legal counsel and relied upon everything his legal counsel told him to do, such is a basis for eliminating the employee's claim for punitive damages before the matter ever goes to trial. This is why in many situations, employers either have highly trained Human Resource Specialists investigate sexual harassment complaints, with the advice of counsel, or have legal counsel investigate such matters directly.

> *"Lawyer: one who protects us against robbery*
> *by taking away the temptation."*
> —H. L. Mencken

Step #22: Understand that Litigation Is Generally Based on Economics, Not Justice or Fairness (see Section 3.0)

> *"Despite the cost of living, it's still popular."*
> —Lawrence J. Peter

Step #23: Utilize Insurance Options

These days, there is basically insurance available for nearly every type of situation one could imagine. Not too long ago, it was reported that some nuns had applied for an insurance policy whereby if they succeeded in bearing a child through Immaculate Conception, the policy would provide for the care and well being of that child. Initially, the insurance company actually granted the policy, but thereafter changed its mind. Consequently, insurance is pretty much available for anything.

There are policies referred to as employer's professional liability (commonly referred to as EPL policies). Under these policies, the carrier will typically retain legal counsel for the boss and/or supervisor regarding wrongful termination and/or discrimination lawsuits brought against either the boss or the supervisor while working in the course and scope of his employment. The premiums on these policies are not cheap in that frequently the attorney's fees and costs in such matters of course can be in the six-digit numbers, but at the same time are available so as to avoid a company from going out of business in having to hire an attorney to defend such litigation. These policies will also usually have what are referred to as indemnification provisions wherein if the employee does recover some type of damages, the insurance carrier will pay for those damages with the exception of punitive damages. Under most laws (state, federal, and foreign), it is against public policy for an insurance company to cover an employer for punitive damages. (See Section 1.3.) (It is similar to having insurance coverage for engaging in criminal activity.)

Most larger entities have EPL coverage, whereas most Mom and Pop businesses cannot afford that luxury and take the risk. Carefully evaluate whether or not this is an option that you want to explore.

You can buy insurance for pretty much anything.
In the 1700s, England had arrangements where it was possible
to obtain insurance against going to hell.

Step #24: Properly Handle the Termination of an Employee's Employment (see Section 10.0)

QUESTIONABLE TERMINATION?
A part-time busboy at a restaurant in California captured a thief who had robbed one of the restaurant's customers in the men's room.
The busboy was terminated for fighting and leaving work.
—Encyclopedia Brown's Book of Strange Facts

Step #25: Use Time Clocks for Hourly Employees

Frequently claims are brought by employees asserting that they are not paid all the overtime to which they are entitled, nor are they given their full lunch or the two ten-minute breaks to which they are entitled under applicable law, and/or related hourly claims. When these arise, employees often file claims with local governmental agencies, alleging violation of wage and hour laws wherein they can recover not only for the hours for which they were not compensated, but also the penalties for the failure to timely pay such wages. In some instances, the employees can recover their attorney's fees.

Oftentimes the penalties in these types of cases outweigh substantially the amount of the actual overtime that was not paid. It also is not unusual for these types of actions to be brought as a class action, which can get quite expensive. (Imagine all of the employees who have worked for you for the last four years receiving a notice that they are entitled to recover money against you if you did not pay them all the money to which they were entitled for overtime, etc.) When this occurs by way of a class action, all the employees who have been disgruntled over the last three or four years are climbing out of the woodwork to come after you, and therefore the best defense in this situation is avoidance. The judges and the administrative officers handling these types of cases take the position that the burden is upon the employer for failure to pay overtime and/or all of the wages and compensation to which the employee is entitled.

For a variety of reasons, employers do not use time clocks. One reason is that either they or their employees feel that such is demeaning to the employees. In such cases, either no time cards are kept, or the time frames are simply written in on the time cards and initialed by the supervisor. Employees voice complaints that for them to have to fill out a time card means that the employer does not trust them.

Without being too blunt, the reality is that most employers and supervisors do not trust employees when it comes to this topic and/or frequently employers and supervisors abuse the overtime laws. If as an employer or supervisor you are required to defend yourself for failure to pay overtime, and you do not use a system that cannot be altered, such as a time clock, then usually the judge or the administrative judge will take the position that you, the employer or supervisor, have failed to meet the burden required by law. Often the judge or jury will find in favor for the employee, especially in those situations wherein the employee brings in a calendar claiming that she has been writing down, for her own records, the amount of hours that she has normally worked. When the applicable statute of limitations in these cases typically runs three to four years, and the employee claims that she has been working thirty minutes to an hour every day without receiving overtime compensation, these amounts, when spread out among all of your employees, can add up to a substantial sum.

The bottom line: make sure you use time clocks that cannot be altered.

The average workweek prior to 1861
was eleven hours a day at six days a week.

Step #26: Select Qualified Legal Counsel and Human Resources Personnel (see Section 11.0)

Twenty-six of the forty-two men elected U.S. president
have been lawyers.

Step #27: Follow the Golden Rule of Employment

The rules and laws regarding criminal matters, contract matters, real estate matters, and most other areas of the law, first began literally thousands of years ago. On the other hand, the laws regarding employment (for the most part) occurred within the last few decades and continue to be the most rapidly changing and evolving areas of the law in the world today. Consequently, it is impossible for any person to keep up with all of the laws and changes. To try and address this problem, in this book you are provided with some rather simplified approaches in dealing with employees, which allows you (as opposed to some litigation-crazed employees and their attorneys) to determine who will be residing in your home next year. One rather simple rule to follow is called "The Golden Rule of Employment." Simply stated, "Do unto employees as you would have them do unto you." This includes all aspects of the employment relationship not only in the area of *respect*, but also in the areas of being fair and reasonable.

"Every man is guilty of all the good he didn't do."
—Voltaire

Tact was defined by Abraham Lincoln as
"the ability to describe others as they see themselves."

Step #28: Avoid Combining Employees and Alcohol

Christmas holidays are oftentimes my most profitable time of the season. More specifically, there are a multitude of employers who commingle their company's Christmas parties or holiday parties with alcohol. Alcohol has done more to purchase my automobiles and make my house payments than most any other employer act that I can think of.

These days, to make the situation even worse for bosses and supervisors is the fact that usually at these holiday festivities, there is someone there with either a digital or video camera documenting all inappropriate and improper acts that are taking place.

For whatever reason, many bosses and supervisors have the mistaken belief that in essence their conduct at such festivities is not something for which they can be held responsible. They are under the mistaken belief that attendance at such gatherings is voluntary and therefore not the responsibility of the employer, which is simply untrue. Almost without exception, it is the argument asserted by the employees at these gatherings that they felt in essence pressured or forced to attend such activities. Even if such is not the case, if the supervisor is involved with and/or is permitting inappropriate conduct to take place toward his employees at such activities (most likely involving actions of sexual harassment, etc.), the company is responsible whether or not the employee attended voluntarily.

The other most common factor that arises is the after-hour visit by supervisors and subordinates to the local pub. Frequently, and all too frequently, this results in claims of sexual harassment as more specifically referenced in Section 6.0, et seq.

Bottom line: from a legal standpoint, mixing alcohol and work is simply a bad idea, whether it is at holiday parties, after-hour get-togethers, company picnics, or any other similar matter. On top of the foregoing, there of course are claims that if someone is under the influence of anything while working in the course and scope of his employment, that such is not only negligence, but constitutes at a minimum, gross negligence and perhaps even intentional misconduct. Consequently if any injuries arise as a result of an employee being under the influence, the liability and exposure is enormous, which in most cases will not be covered by any type of insurance.

"What I don't like about office Christmas parties
is looking for a job the next day."
—Phyllis Diller

Step #29: Treat Temporary Employees Like They Are Your Own Because They May Well Be (see Section 4.4)

Step #30: Wisely Handle Communications with Employees' Representatives

With litigation and employment disputes continually on the increase, it is not that unusual anymore for the boss or supervisor to be contacted by an employee's representative, whether it be a union representative or legal representative. Oftentimes, I have had clients who have simply fired their employees for retaining legal counsel, or at a minimum, certainly treating them differently because of such actions. In some states, including California, it is unlawful for a boss or supervisor to treat an employee differently because that employee has retained the services of a representative to discuss the conditions of the employee's employment.

If you have employees who have a collective bargaining agreement, of course it is mandated contractually that their representatives speak on their behalf regarding their employment situations; and any retaliation is not only a violation of the contract, but in addition constitutes a tort in violation of public policy justifying tort damages as referenced in Sections 1.1 through 1.6.

All too frequently, employers will sometimes have the spouse or parents of their employees try and speak on the employee's behalf that, absent some written authorization from the employee, is totally inappropriate and likewise should be avoided. These types of communications also make it difficult for the boss or supervisor to determine whether or not he has a right to unilaterally communicate directly with the employee. In most instances, it is helpful to make sure there is something in writing confirming such authorization, and even when that does occur, such does not mean that the boss or supervisor is precluded from communicating directly with the employee so as to make sure the employee is properly doing his or her job duties and responsibilities.

Simply put, a boss or supervisor is not required to go through an employee's attorney in order to communicate with the employee regarding the employee properly performing the employee's job duties and responsibilities. If at any time you as a boss or supervisor receive instructions from the employee's representative that you are to cease all communications with the employee directly (which would include ceasing communications about doing the job duties and responsibilities or ceasing to be able to continue to supervise the employee in doing his or her duties and responsibilities), you should request that such demands be put in writing and immediately consult with legal counsel. I would anticipate that most attorneys would instruct you that you may well be within your rights to terminate that individual's employment.

Once again any time an employee retains the services of some representative to speak on his or her behalf, it is a good idea to make sure that you are speaking with your legal representative before taking any action.

Step #31: Put Thorough Documentation in Personnel Files

One of the first things I do in every case that our firm defends is to ask the boss or supervisor to provide a copy of the employee's personnel file to our office. This is also one of the first things that the governmental agencies researching claims of discrimination and/or wrongful termination request, whether it be the Equal Employment Opportunity Commission, Department of Fair Employment and Housing for the State of California, or such similar organization. The reason why the personnel file is so important is that it presumably is the best evidence of whatever defenses the employer has with regard to any and all actions taken by the boss or supervisor toward the employee.

You can well imagine the impact that occurs in a situation where an employee might have worked for several years and is fired and who claims some type of discrimination, yet when either the governmental agencies or I request a copy of the personnel file, there is absolutely nothing in that file. That is not something that either the judge or jury are particularly happy about in that both state, federal, and foreign law mandate that it is the employer's obligation to maintain documentation regarding such actions. If he or she does not have the documentation, the most likely effect is that it will be perceived by either the governmental agencies, or the judges and juries in such matters, that the employee's claim of discrimination or wrongful termination or related assertions is valid.

It is not unusual in many of the cases that our firm has handled that the only thing that is in the employee's personnel file (following a termination) is some glowing letter of recommendation which the boss or supervisor issued because she felt guilty about having to fire the employee. On the other hand, the employee oftentimes has a three-ring binder full of documentation, color-coded, indexed and alphabetized, listing for the last three or four years everything unlawful that the employer has done. Imagine that you are sitting as a juror on such case and what type of an impact this would have upon you.

Unless you have agreed through a collective bargaining agreement or some such similar document, there is no requirement that every time you put a document in an employee's personnel file, the employee is automatically entitled to see such at that time. There are some laws that require employers to provide to employees, upon reasonable notice, copies of all documentation that they have signed or that are maintained in their personnel files with certain exceptions. Accordingly, there is really little or no excuse for employers not to have a properly documented personnel file on every employee, especially if they are taking some type of negative action toward any employee. Remember, IF IT IS NOT IN WRITING, IT WAS NOT SAID.

Also, remember that the purpose of documentation is to confirm what you have told your employees verbally. It makes little or no sense to document somebody's personnel file without telling the employee about a deficiency as well. It is not required that you have an employee sign everything that goes into his personnel file. However, depending upon the nature of the situation, you may well want to have the employee sign an acknowledgment of the documentation so as to confirm that this is indeed a serious matter. If you face a situation where an employee fails to sign a simple acknowledgment or receipt of documentation, let him know that such insubordination may in and of itself be grounds for termination of his employment, which you would like to avoid. Remember, if you are going to require employees to sign acknowledgment forms, just like anything else be consistent.

Employment inconsistency is the foundation
upon which employment litigation is built.

"The palest ink is better than the best memory."
—Chinese Proverb

Section 3.0

Litigation is Generally Controlled by Economics, Not Justice or Fairness

While fairness and justice are considerations for the jury, the simple realities are that in order for an employee to assert a claim for wrongful termination and/or discrimination, she has one of two choices. The first choice is that she can pay an attorney on an hourly basis for the attorney's services. This option is rarely followed because the costs of attorney's fees in these types of cases oftentimes are in the six-digit numbers.

Consequently, the realities of litigation are that an employee cannot pursue a lawsuit unless she can convince an attorney to take the lawsuit on what is referred to as a "contingency" fee basis. Most contingency fee cases relating to employment matters are arrangements whereby the employee is not required to pay any attorney's fees unless and until the employee actually prevails in the litigation or the case is settled. Under such circumstances, the attorney typically receives one-third of the recovery if the matter is resolved before going to trial and oftentimes will receive as much as forty percent of the recovery if the case results in a jury verdict or settles after trial has commenced. In most instances, the employee is still obligated to pay the costs of litigation, which includes the filing costs, expert costs, the court reporter costs, travel costs, etc. These costs are typically fronted by the employee's attorney, and then reimbursed to the employee's attorney if the case is ruled in favor of the employee. If the case does not result in favor of the employee, then the attorney has the right to pursue the employee for such costs (other than the attorney's fees). In most such instances, however, the employee does not have any assets and therefore the attorney frequently waives pursuing such fees.

This is the reason why employment cases are oftentimes difficult to settle. Once an employee has convinced an attorney to take her case, there is little or no incentive (other than the fear of losing) for the employee to dismiss the case or settle the case for some nuisance value before it goes to a jury trial, wherein the possibilities of a huge judgment may occur.

A screening process normally takes place regarding all lawsuits brought by a plaintiff's attorney, wherein the plaintiff's attorney determines in advance whether or not the case is one he wants to take on a contingency fee basis before filing the lawsuit. This screening process is even more stringent on employment matters, in that the cost and time that the employee's attorney will incur are significantly higher than most other forms of litigation, such as automobile accidents, slip-and-fall cases, medical malpractice, etc. Employment cases have typically longer depositions, as well as many experts, plus the trials last substantially longer. This all means more money that the employee's attorney is gambling in hope that the "Blue-Haired Lady" will be sympathetic toward the employee.

Accordingly, the next time you hear an employee threaten litigation, such is really meaningless unless he can convince an attorney to take his case. There is no shortage in this world of disgruntled employees who are unhappy with their bosses and supervisors. The challenge for the employee is to find an attorney who is willing to risk taking the employee's lawsuit on a contingency fee basis. Keep in mind that it usually is much better for the boss or supervisor to resolve an employee matter before it gets to the stage wherein the employee starts looking for an attorney.

Consequently, always take the threat of litigation seriously. As a general rule, try to resolve such disputes promptly with the employee directly, where reasonably possible. PUT ANOTHER WAY, IF YOU KNOW YOU ARE WRONG, SWALLOW YOUR PRIDE AND REMEDY THE SITUATION AS SOON AS POSSIBLE. Usually in most discrimination cases, once an attorney gets involved on behalf of the employee (and you either settle or unfortunately lose the case), you will usually not only be compensating the employee for all of her losses but also paying for her attorney.

MOST EMPLOYEES' ATTORNEYS ARE LOOKING FOR AN EMPLOYEE WHO WILL BE VIEWED WITH SYMPATHY, in that these are typically the most profitable cases. It is for this reason that of the multitude of forms of unlawful discrimination that exist, employees' attorneys tend to limit the types of cases they take to only certain classifications of discrimination. This is because it is the employees' attorney's perception in most instances that the "Blue-Haired Ladies" (see Step #2) may not be that sympathetic toward all plaintiffs.

A good example of this includes sexual harassment cases. In general, sexual harassment cases by females against males are very popular amongst employees' attorneys (see Section 6.0). FREQUENTLY, MALE ATTENDEES POINT OUT TO ME IN MY SEMINARS THAT THEY TOO CAN BE SEXUALLY HARASSED, WHICH IS TRUE, BUT IN REALITY RARELY DOES ANYONE CARE. Employees' attorneys, particularly where the female supervisor is attractive, rarely take a sexual harassment case by a male against a female supervisor. In such matters, the employees' attorney's worst nightmare is that they might spend tens of thousands of dollars of their own time and money on such a case, while their male client is breaking down emotionally on the witness stand discussing how he was sexually harassed by his voluptuous supervisor. At the same time the males in the jury box are giving high fives to each other thinking that the male employee was lucky. While such sexist analogies are not politically correct, they are often accurate. Bosses and supervisors should still aggressively protect males, as well as individuals of the same and opposite sex from any form of sexual harassment. There are economic realities, however, which make some cases more attractive than others.

These economic realities are important for bosses and supervisors to remember, in that such are for the most part what determines whether or not the plaintiff's attorney will take the case. Consequently, when I receive calls relating to a particular employment situation from a boss or supervisor, my goal is to eliminate as much as reasonably possible any legal liability in the matter. In doing so, I keep several things in mind, typically in the following order:

A. The law on the given subject

B. The "Blue-Haired Lady doctrine"

C. "The Golden Rule of Employment"

D. Make sure that the method of handling the situation is the least possibly attractive to an employee's potential attorney.

"Leave it to a girl to take the fun out of sex discrimination."
—Bill Watterson in his comic strip, *Calvin & Hobbes*

Section 4.0

Interviewing and Screening Applicants for Employment

Proper interviewing and screening is one of the most effective and efficient methods of reducing a boss and supervisor's liability. While most states recognize the legal theory of wrongful refusal to hire, the reality is that few employees' attorneys will take such cases, in that these do not make particularly sympathetic cases with juries. Most "Blue-Haired Ladies" perceive that if the applicant is prohibited from getting a job at one place of employment, all she needs to do is go down the road and get a job elsewhere. Therefore, it's simply not that big of a deal not to hire someone, regardless of the employer's motivation.

Keep in mind, however, if the boss or supervisor is flagrant in his refusal to hire, it is still quite possible to raise the ire of the "Blue-Haired Ladies." Therefore, do not assume this is your golden opportunity to ignore discrimination laws. ALL TOO FREQUENTLY BOSSES AND SUPERVISORS WALK THE LITIGATION TIGHTROPE AND FALL.

Remember the goal in interviewing is
to get the right person for the right job.
As Mark Twain once stated:
"Thousands of geniuses live and die undiscovered
—either by themselves or by others."

All too many times, bosses and supervisors get into gray areas and think that because they can come up with some reasonable factual rationalization for whatever position they are taking, that they are okay. Frequently, they ask their attorneys if under a particular factual scenario they are okay from a legal standpoint, without necessarily always disclosing all of the material facts, oftentimes resulting in their obtaining from their attorneys the answer they want to hear.

The reality, however, is that in most factual disputes, it is going to be up to a "Blue-Haired Lady" (who will hear both sides) to determine whether or not she believes the supervisor or the employee. Keep in mind juries have substantial discretion in what they decide. Therefore, it is very difficult, if not impossible, for an attorney to accurately predict the outcome of all such situations. This is particularly true because in many instances the boss or supervisor, either intentionally or through lack of understanding, failed to fully disclose all relevant information to his attorney; or on the other hand, the attorney with whom he is consulting is not really qualified.

The bottom line: it is far better to refuse to hire someone at the beginning, as opposed to hiring her and terminating her later. Your liability goes up exponentially after you have actually hired an individual and then fire her. Remember, that in a refuse-to-hire case the potential damage categories, including loss of wages, punitive damages, damage for emotional distress, and attorney's fees (in discrimination claims), are the same as in a wrongful termination case.

DEFINITION OF EQUAL RIGHTS:
"Everyone will have a fair chance at being incompetent. "
—Laurence J. Peter

Section 4.1: Advertising for Applicants

An effective manner to get the word out that you are looking to hire an employee is to advertise. Alternatives for such include newspapers, the media in general, the Internet, headhunters, word-of-mouth and a host of other options. Be extremely careful on the wording that goes into your advertisements. You should not make any representation relating to the expected duration of the individual's employment. Accordingly, avoid the use of terms such as "permanent," "long term," etc., in that such language can convincingly be argued as a waiver of the "at will" doctrine. Advertisements are not a good place to be specific about the applicant's job duties and responsibilities, in that such would normally be included in job descriptions (see Section 4.2). Further, make all language in the advertisement neutral, so as to avoid any references as to sex, age, race, religion, marital status, disability, gender, sexual orientation, and/or any other protected classifications.

Section 4.2: Job Descriptions

In going through the interviewing and screening process, it is most important to have, in advance of any interview, a detailed job description. This permits the boss and/or supervisor to show the job description to the applicant during the interview. This will be helpful in allowing the applicant to determine whether or not he or she perceives that he or she will have any difficulties or complications in performing the job duties and responsibilities specified in the description.

AVOID THE USE OF JOB DESCRIPTIONS THAT ARE GENERAL OR VAGUE IN SUBSTANCE, SUCH AS SIMPLY STATING, "DO SUCH JOBS AS ARE ASSIGNED." These types of job descriptions fail to give notice to the employee of what is expected of the employee. Accordingly, this gives the employee an excellent excuse and justification to oppose your criticism of that individual for performance reasons when you failed to specify what the employee was supposed to perform.

Generalized job descriptions frequently backfire on an employer, particularly when the employer attempts to take the position that because of some type of illness or injury the employee is no longer able to do the job and therefore must be terminated. The employee in such situations usually will point to the job description, indicating that there is nothing in the job description specifying that his or her current injury or illness would prevent him from being able to do what is set forth in the job description.

Accordingly, make sure the job description sets forth in detail the physical requirements of the job, as well as a clear outline of what you would want to know if you were going to be doing the job. The description should include references to all physical and mental abilities that are required for the job such as 20/20 vision, full auditory abilities, as well as average intelligence—or above, if necessary. Further in the description you can specify and put in language as to whether or not the job is exempt or non-exempt.

Remember, if you are going to claim that the position is exempt, it is helpful to specify in the job description the type of duties that are normally considered to be exempt. Claiming that an employee is exempt and then having a job description specifying that they will be doing manual work or such language as clerical, typing, etc. are inconsistent with exempt status; and therefore, this is the time to make sure that you have properly classified your employee.

Section 4.3: The Job Interview

THE INTERVIEW IS A PROCESS WHERE NOT ONLY THE BOSS OR SUPERVISOR INTERVIEWS THE EMPLOYEE, BUT IT ALSO IS AN OPPORTUNITY TO SELL THE EMPLOYEE ON THE EMPLOYER. Usually the best employer/employee relationships are those comprised of mutual *respect* and benefit. Employers that have both will typically be able to recruit employees over their competition. Therefore, employee marketing starts even before the employee is hired. Hopefully, the employer can convince the employee that it is indeed a privilege and an honor to work for that particular employer and is not just a job.

During the interviewing process, be *respectful* of the applicant; and at all times remember the "Golden Rule of Employment." Do not make the applicant wait in the reception area needlessly, and do not monopolize the few precious moments you have during the interview by requiring the applicant to be exposed to your worldviews. If done properly, the applicant should be talking approximately ninety percent of the time. Keep in mind, you have anywhere from seven to thirty minutes during an average interview to try and determine whether or not this is the type of person you may work well with for the next few decades. Make the most of this opportunity.

> *"It's difficult to keep quiet if you have nothing to say."*
> *—Malcolm Margolin*

Section 4.3(a): Questions During the Interview

In determining what types of questions to ask during the interviewing process, please keep in mind that the law generally balances the right of the employer to ask the question versus the employee's right of privacy. Consequently, there may well be a multitude of things you may like to know about the employee, which the courts and legislature have determined are outweighed by the employee's right of privacy.

For example, it is relevant for you as a boss or supervisor to know whether the applicant has ever filed a workers' compensation case before. On the other hand, the courts have made it very clear that your right to know is outweighed by the employee's right of privacy and therefore this is an inappropriate question to ask.

As a general rule, stay away from any questions which are in any manner related to the traditionally protected classifications under employment law, such as questions regarding age, sex, marital status, race, religion, sexual orientation, medical condition, disability, national origin, pregnancy, etc.

There are a few limited situations where you do have a right to go into some of these categories, such as if you were the employer interviewing to fill the position of the Pope, it is permissible to ask if that applicant is Catholic. Keep in mind, however, the law is very protective of an employee's rights of privacy.

There are several questions that are entirely appropriate. ONE OF THE BEST QUESTIONS IS TO ASK THE APPLICANT HIS OR HER PERCEPTIONS OF HIS OR HER OWN STRENGTHS AND WEAKNESSES. It is recommended to start the interviewing process with something a little less confrontational, however, such as simply asking the applicant to talk about him or herself. Many governmental agencies strongly recommend asking open-ended questions; however, the realities are that applicants will frequently give you much more information than you need or have a right to know. It is important, however, that you make your employment determination on a nondiscriminatory and lawful basis. Accordingly, if an applicant volunteers to you that he has a rather unique religion it is advisable for you not to ask follow-up questions about such. It is likewise important to remember the type of job that the applicant is interviewing for. If you are interviewing an individual to become an attorney, the line of questioning and the manner in which you address the individual will significantly vary from an individual who is applying to shovel manure (although frequently the jobs are viewed as being very similar in nature). In general, "Blue-Haired Ladies" understand that the line of questioning may well vary depending upon the job requirements.

Remember to find out about their background.
As Julius Caesar stated:
"Experience is the teacher of all things."

No matter how poorly an applicant does during an interview, do not cut the interview short. Keep in mind the "Golden Rule of Employment," and also REMEMBER THAT THE PERSON YOU INTERVIEW TODAY MAY BE INTERVIEWING YOU TOMORROW. Further, this person has the potential of either talking positively or negatively about you in your own business community. Typically your business community is very small, and therefore you have a reputation you want to protect.

At the end of the interview, always let the applicant know when you will get back to her with a decision and make sure you get back to her within a reasonable time and don't just leave her hanging.

Make sure somewhere during the interview you have asked the applicant whether or not she is qualified and can do the job duties and responsibilities set forth in the job description. Additionally, make sure you ask her about why it is she left any and all of her prior jobs and whether or not she is willing to provide to you any references from each and every one of those prior jobs. If not, a red flag should go up.

Also question her about any gaps of any kind that exist in her employment history, as well as asking her why she believes she would be the best candidate to fill your job opening. Also ask what, if anything, she knows about your company, as well as giving her an opportunity to question you about the company or the job. At no time during the interviewing process tell her how she has done versus other candidates, nor make any type of representations to her as to whether or not she has the job.

Once again, "buying time" is helpful under these circumstances, even if it is only a day, in that you will want to check out references. Typically hiring on the spot is more beneficial for the employee than it is for the boss or supervisor.

FOUR DISASTERS IN JOB INTERVIEWING

1. *One applicant asked the interviewer to engage in arm wrestling.*
2. *One applicant said that he had failed to finish high school following his kidnapping and being locked in a closet in the country of Mexico.*
3. *A bald applicant left the interview and then came back wearing a full toupee.*
4. *This applicant contacted her therapist during the interview for recommendations.*
   —From <u>Parade Magazine</u>

Remember, applicants will communicate to others how you treated them, and thus your reputation is at stake.

> *"Glass, china, and reputation are easily cracked,*
> *and never mended well."*
> *—Benjamin Franklin*

"A reputation once broken may possibly be repaired,
but the world will always keep their eyes
on the spot where the crack was."
—Joseph Hall

Section 4.4: Alternative Personnel Arrangements

Many employers look to alternatives to direct hiring, hoping to avoid and reduce liability, increase benefits, and also avoid the complications of handling payroll. Additionally some employers do not want the overhead cost of employing a human resources person, or simply believe alternative hiring arrangements will alleviate many of the general hassles that go along with acting as an employer. In many instances, this is most effective. In other situations, it can actually create more problems than it solves.

If the sole reason you are seeking to utilize an employment agency or obtain personnel through a contracted personnel or management company is to avoid liability regarding discrimination or wrongful termination, such justification is without merit in most instances. More specifically, the laws in most jurisdictions recognize that discrimination applies to not only the employer and employee relationship, but also many other relationships, including temporary personnel and employment relationships through management companies. Additionally, if you have some control over the employee (which occurs in most of these situations), the law will imply a joint employer liability theory. Under this approach, not only is the management company or temporary employment agency responsible, but so are you. Many employers utilize temporary employment services and/or contracted personnel companies for only a portion of their work force. This may be another alternative you might want to explore.

The success or lack thereof regarding these alternatives varies as much as the different types of fields of employment that exist. At a minimum, if you wanted to utilize the services of a management company or temporary employment agency, make sure you have a written contract with that organization (preferably reviewed and approved by your own qualified attorney). It is certainly a good idea to have a provision in the contract wherein the boss and/or supervisor are held harmless as much as reasonably possible under the circumstances and indemnified for any liability that might arise through the relationship. In reality, most management companies will not agree to such, in that it is their understandable position that they cannot control how you treat these individuals, and therefore it would not be fair or reasonable to hold you harmless from your own conduct.

It is a good idea to make sure that the management company or lease company with whom you are dealing is fiscally sound or at least insured or bonded, as opposed to being located next to the meat section in your local supermarket. Otherwise, under the joint employer liability theories that exist, the employee will simply come after you for the wrongdoing of the management company, which is not something you want to have occur. Feel free to obtain references from these companies to see how successfully they are servicing their customers.

As it relates to the topic of independent contractors, for whatever reason many bosses and supervisors believe they can avoid basically all forms of liability regarding most all laws, including wrongful termination, discrimination, workers' compensation and income taxes, as well as payroll taxes, because they choose to call the persons working for them independent contractors. All too frequently, such bosses and supervisors assume that because the person who is working for them agreed to such, it must be legal, which is simply not the case.

Labor Boards throughout the United States are clamping down hard on these types of relationships. There is significant liability and exposure for such. As a general rule, if you exercise significant control over the individual, regardless of what you call him, he is an employee. A multitude of employers force individuals to become independent contractors, oftentimes resulting in abuses of overtime, failure to pay social security, unemployment benefits, workers' compensation insurance, etc. Once the government finds out that such abuse has taken place, they have no humor about such and are inclined to make an example of such employers by going back over several years in requiring not only back pay and benefits to the individual involved, but also looking at your relationship with all the other individuals with whom you are working. They also have the option of adding significant and substantial penalties and also potentially criminal sanctions. This approach is not only in the gray zone; it has fallen off into the red zone and the odds are quite high (especially when your relationship with this worker ceases) that said workers are going to report you. They will be able to get three years or more worth of compensation and benefits that they would have gotten had you actually treated them as employees.

"One machine can do the combined work of fifty ordinary men. . .
There is no machine that can do the work
of one extraordinary man."
—Elbert Hubbard

Section 4.5: Interview Documentation, Selection, and Notification

As it relates to documentation, keep in mind that most states require employers to maintain employment applications and interview materials for three or more years, depending on the state involved. Be careful, however, about what you put on the documentation.

One case handled by a law firm several years ago involved a claim by an employee that she was discriminated against and not hired because she was pregnant, which was adamantly denied by the employer, who also denied knowing she was pregnant. In this particular case, the employer did properly maintain the interviewing documentation and records; however, unfortunately for the employer, the employer's notes taken during the interview had the word "PREGNANT" written upon them. Such notations are not particularly helpful in defending discrimination cases, as one can well imagine.

In order to avoid any misunderstanding of your intentions regarding the applicant for a job, consider using either an alphabetical (similar to giving grades from A to F) or a numeric system of 1 through 10, to keep track of where you rate a particular applicant. Destruction of such documents and/or materials carries with it substantial penalties, and also if the matter goes before a jury, creates substantial prejudice against you in the mind of the "Blue-Haired Lady."

As to providing notification to an applicant following an interview, this can simply be done by way of a standard diplomatically written letter. THERE IS NO REQUIREMENT FOR YOU TO SPECIFY WHY A PARTICULAR INDIVIDUAL WAS NOT SELECTED FOR A PARTICULAR POSITION. Rather indicate to him or her that it was deemed he or she was not the person best qualified for the job. If the applicant calls you back and asks for details or specifics, be consistent in your responses again by simply indicating that he or she was not the best person qualified for the job in your opinion. Do not in any manner deviate from this response.

Additionally, avoid giving commentary on how well or not an individual handled the interviewing process. Frequently applicants will call up indicating that they want feedback, so as not to make the same mistakes twice. From a legal standpoint, it is not recommended that you get into such a dialogue. These types of conversations can lead to agitation and unhappiness, as well as potential litigation. Your job as an interviewer is not to give lessons to the applicant on how to participate and respond during the interview process. Furthermore, whatever you say could well be misunderstood or misquoted, and therefore going into such a dialogue is not recommended.

Many employee attorneys have directed their clients to inquire of a boss or supervisor who rejected their clients as to the basis for said rejection. Frequently employees use the approach of indicating that they simply want to improve their interview skills (and in some instances this is probably true).

Bottom line: don't fall into this trap. Your job is not to educate individuals on how to handle themselves during an interview.

*A person who is afraid of work is referred to as an
"ergasiophobe."*

Section 4.6: References, Background, and Medical Examinations

It is always advisable before actually making a job offer that it be preconditioned upon the applicant's satisfactorily passing a background or reference check. Background checks are typically much more detailed than a reference check, which normally involves calling up an applicant's prior employer. Typically, supervisors indicate to successful applicants that they can have the job, subject to their satisfactorily completing a reference or background check. In doing reference checks, always try and contact the person's immediate supervisor. They typically will have a better feel for the applicant than will the human resources department of the applicant's prior employer and will typically be more open and honest in their responses.

Most employers, if they are smart, have written policies and procedures precluding supervisors and managers from giving out any references without going through the human resources department. (This is again a policy you should have in your personnel manual.) This does not, however, mean that you need to follow such rules in obtaining information for yourself. If you can find a supervisor or manager who is willing to share information with you, take advantage of the opportunity.

Keep in mind as well that when you are being questioned about references for individuals, there is also the possibility of you being personally sued for a violation of their right of privacy and/or defamation. Some states have statutes wherein you can be sued if you misrepresent anything about an employee's prior employment history. Therefore from your standpoint, there is little incentive to give out any information. In such cases, advise the inquiring potential employer that you are not permitted to disclose such information, pursuant to your company's policies and procedures. It is recommended to my clients that they only confirm hiring and termination dates. DO NOT address whether or not the individual is re-hirable.

When checking references, it is a good idea to make sure that the applicant knows that you are going to be taking such action. Many bosses or supervisors call applicant's present supervisors only to find out that her present supervisor was unaware of the fact that she was seeking a job. This is not exactly getting off on the right foot with the applicant; therefore be cautious in your inquiries.

Finally, in some jurisdictions including California, there are now rules that if you obtain any background information about an applicant, you have an obligation under specific circumstances to disclose that information to the applicant. Therefore you ought to be familiar with your jurisdiction's laws as it relates to this matter.

Some companies employ outside investigation agencies to conduct reference and/or background checks. For whatever reason, many employers feel that because these companies conduct these checks, that the employer has no liability or responsibility for the information that is obtained, which is simply untrue. Whenever such companies are conducting background or reference checks regarding an applicant, they are working as an agent for you the employer; and therefore the employer, and in some instances arguably the supervisor, will be liable for the actions of these agencies. Make sure that you have a carefully worded written contract between your company and such investigation agencies to make sure that they hold you harmless from any unlawful conduct they engage in; and make sure they have the financial ability so as to back up any such claims. Also, check out their references with their customers to make sure that they have some credibility.

As it relates to the topic of pre-employment physical examinations, such are not universally permitted under all state, federal, and foreign laws. Once again a balancing of the employee's right of privacy versus the employer's right to know is involved. If the applicant is applying for a nursing position, the right to conduct a pre-employment physical is generally permissible. On the other hand, conducting a complete pre-employment physical for a typist might be questionable. Under such circumstances, it might be argued that the reason you are doing such it to determine whether or not the applicant has any pre-existing physical conditions which might make her more likely to file a workers' compensation claim, and/or allows you to find out information about her medical condition, which these days is typically forbidden. Additionally, keep in mind that there are new laws, both state, federal, and foreign, imposing substantial penalties on bosses and supervisors for disclosing information about applicants' and employees' medical conditions and records, so be very careful in this area.

While prior to the 1950s, most individuals held two different jobs; nowadays the average worker in the United States will have had eight different jobs by the time they reach forty years of age.

Section 4.7: Pre-Employment Testing

There are varieties of tests that various employers provide to applicants.

One of the most popular is pre-employment drug testing, which is pretty much accepted so long as the request to take the test is preceded by a conditional job offer. Furthermore, such is allowed so long as the test is consistently applied. Accordingly, no matter how justified (and I am speaking as an individual who is partially Irish), it would be discriminatory under both state, federal, and foreign law to conduct drug testing on only Irish applicants, although probably justified.

Additionally the common practice of having policies of testing individuals who appear to be under the influence of some type of drug or alcohol (commonly referred to as "for-cause drug testing") is universally allowed under state, federal, and foreign law, as are drug and alcohol tests that occur following accidents (also see Step #28).

Random drug testing on the other hand (examples include putting all the employees names in a jar and see whose name comes up that month, so as to make a deposit into the urinalysis jar) is not legally permissible. More specifically, these types of tests are viewed as crossing the gray line into the red line regarding the violation of the employee's right of privacy. There is an exception of certain employees who operate certain equipment, such as large trucks, etc. who are covered by the rules and regulations of the federal government, and specifically the Department of Transportation (i.e., D.O.T.). The D.O.T. mandates random drug testing of such individuals. It is, however, required in most states that the employees be advised in advance of any drug testing that they will be subjected to.

Therefore, it is imperative to make sure the drug testing policies and procedures are in the employee's handbook, and further, that they have signed waiver agreements allowing them to be tested. Keep in mind the liability in conducting drug testing is not in the testing itself, but rather in what action you take if an individual fails the test, or if you disclose such information to third persons. While some employers might be prone to give an employee another chance, such action creates its own problems, in that if you allow a Baptist employee a second chance, you had better do the same for every other religion and non-religion, or they could claim religious discrimination, etc.

As you can see, inconsistencies are what oftentimes lead to discrimination claims. Accordingly, as a general rule (from a legal standpoint) it is better to consistently terminate all employees who fail drug or alcohol tests, so long as you are sure that the testing was done properly.

As referenced above, another area of liability regarding these tests is the requirement of confidentiality, both in conducting the test and also the results. All too often, bosses and supervisors violate this right of privacy, or make defamatory remarks about employees who take such tests. Make sure that the testing laboratory utilized has good references, and make sure you have a written contract between you and the testing laboratory. Make sure they are holding you harmless and indemnifying you from any liability they create because of their mishandling of the situation. Additionally, make sure you have competent legal counsel review the same.

Other examples of testing conducted in the workplace include proficiency tests, such as making sure the clerical help are proficient regarding word processing, etc., which again are permissible, so long as they are uniformly applied. Another type of test sometimes given in the workplace is called a "truth and honesty test." Several companies have developed what they view as test questions, which are given to applicants supposedly reflecting whether the applicant is more likely than not to be truthful and honest. These tests have most frequently been applied to individuals who are referred to as "money handlers" who work at banks or credit unions, etc. These are different than the type of aptitude tests that typically circulate in the work force, which are generally permissible, wherein they help determine a particular applicant's abilities in a given field.

Sometimes, truth and honesty tests include questions that violate the employee's right of privacy. It is of course possible that the company that conducts such tests may not be bonded nor have any type of insurance, which leaves the employer exposed legally. It is recommended that 'truth and honesty" tests not be utilized as a general rule. If you do choose to do such, make sure a qualified attorney carefully reviews them. As it relates to aptitude tests, again make sure that the questions do not violate the employee's right of privacy and have them similarly reviewed.

Section 5.0

Specific Strategies to Avoid Specific Circumstances That Could Result in You Losing Your First-Born Young

"Plan for the future because that's where you're going to spend the rest of your life."
—Mark Twain

Section 5.1: Employees Requesting a Raise or Promotion

How you handle this of course differs significantly upon the employee involved, the job involved, as well as the company's financial condition. There are multitudes of publications in existence teaching employees how to approach bosses and supervisors for raises and promotions. There is very little information teaching bosses and supervisors how to handle this situation.

Just because an employee asks you for a raise or promotion should not result in your immediately becoming defensive. Accordingly under these circumstances, do not react immediately, but again always "Buy Time" (see Step #6). Your goal here (assuming this is an employee you want to keep) should be to not only objectively determine what is a fair and reasonable compensation level for this employee, but more importantly making sure that you are able, in a diplomatic fashion, to convince this employee of such as well.

Frequently employees are underpaid and have not received the compensation to which they are entitled. On the other hand, frequently employees are either mistaken as to what the market is, or in the alternative, overstate and/or oversell their level of worth to the employer. For many employees, it takes quite a bit of courage to approach the person who is not only controlling theirs, but also in many instances their family's financial condition. If you treat their requests as nothing more than a nuisance, not only will they feel dejected and neglected, but additionally their incentive to produce will decrease and typically they will start looking elsewhere for employment.

Make sure you're very familiar with your own company's compensation package for your employees. Many times employees may be overlooking certain benefits they receive, which they fail to calculate when comparing their compensation to your competition. Examples of such include the fact that maybe you have a better healthcare plan, or maybe your retirement plan provides greater matching funds than the competition, or perhaps there are many perks which they are not taking into consideration, such as free lunches, use of employer sports tickets, condos, etc.

On the other hand, do not be so arrogant as to not seriously examine whether or not you are in fact competitive. If the employee is smart, he will have done some research and provided to you some justification for either a raise or promotion. Oftentimes his proposal will reflect not only his outstanding performance, but also an offer or potential offer from the competition or general data as to what the competition is paying. Hopefully you already know this information before you are approached. Still, however, advise the employee that you will look into the situation and get back to him, and do so within a reasonable time. (All too many times bosses and supervisors hope the situation will simply go away by ignoring the issue.) Always remember the "golden rule" (see Step #27).

"Never underestimate a man who overestimates himself."
—*Franklin D. Roosevelt*

Accordingly when you come back to the employee after you have conducted your own research based on whatever information he provided, you are in a rather difficult position. First, if it turns out you really were underpaying the employee, you now have to acknowledge such. More importantly, your employee may lose some trust and confidence in your objectivity and/or feel that his request worked once so he might as well try it again in the future and keep on pushing you.

On the other hand, if you truly perceive that your employee is being paid a reasonable amount, you risk the reality of losing this employee under these circumstances, which you frequently do not want to have occur. The answer in most situations is usually a compromise, wherein you do not necessarily give the employee the increase he was looking for, but at the same time give him more than what he was making before with an explanation as to why you believe this is just and fair. Make sure that you have thoroughly and reasonably investigated such.

If on the other hand, you conclude that you simply cannot afford to pay this individual any more, tell him that and explain why. In many instances, there are many factors which employees are not aware of. By you sharing such information with him, it will at least show that you take him seriously. Hopefully you can convey to him that you're not trying to take advantage of him, but you cannot justifiably pay him more.

Be creative. Perhaps there are alternatives other than increases in pay that will satisfy the employee's needs. Frequent examples in this area include a change in job title, access to additional company benefits such as a health spa membership, periodic access to company sporting event tickets, individualized parking spaces, company-paid-for car leases, health care or perhaps increased health care benefits, etc.

In some instances, you will encounter employees who are simply unrealistic in their expectations, both as to their compensation and also as to their abilities. In these situations, let the employees know as diplomatically and constructively as possible that you might have to simply agree to disagree.

If for whatever reason you can't come to some type of mutual arrangement, you still want to part on as friendly terms as is reasonably possible. In many instances, this is a good way to start negotiations. In this manner you've made it clear to the employee that you want to be reasonable, but at the same time are willing, if necessary, to part ways. Most employees really do not want to change jobs because of the fear of the unknown. By approaching the negotiations in this manner, you've made it clear that as a boss and supervisor you're still in control and are willing to part ways, if in your perception the employee is being unreasonable. At the same time, you've worded it in such a way that you can still justifiably alter your position by providing to the employee some additional compensation.

The first employer to give his employees a two-day weekend
was William Wrigley Jr. of Wrigley's Gum fame.

Section 5.2: What Do You Do When You Suspect an Employee Has an Injury or Medical Problem

What are you going to do when one of your best employees walks in and tells you that the prior evening she hurt her arm bowling; however, she has noticed that it is becoming worse as she continues to do her job duties and responsibilities that morning. She says this to you in passing as if it's no big deal; and in fact when you ask her if she can continue working, she tells you that she thinks that she will be able to get through the day, or words to that effect. Under these circumstances, should you allow her to continue working or not? This is again one of those situations where typically the legal answer may well differ from the business answer.

Legally, once you have been put on notice of such, you have an obligation to require that employee to get a qualified physician (which may have to be done at your own cost) to determine whether or not she is able to continue performing her normal job duties and responsibilities, either with or without accommodation. The business answer may well be that you are so backed up on business, you need to have work done that particular day, and therefore you are willing to take the risk for the potential legal liability. Whichever way the decision is made, it's going to be up to you, the boss or supervisor, to make, in that it is you who are taking the risk.

As a general rule, knowingly allowing an individual to continue working for you who has an injury, whether it is work-related or not, constitutes (at a minimum) negligence on your part and subjects you to legal liability both for the employer and arguably the supervisor personally.

Accordingly, it is a good idea to have a written policy in your personnel handbook. Make it clear that whenever someone feels or perceives that he is going to have any limitation on being able to perform his job duties and responsibilities, he immediately notify his supervisor. Additionally, state that typically he will not be able to return back to work absent receiving a letter from a qualified physician indicating that he is able to do so, either with or without accommodations; and if accommodations are required, to specify what they are so your attorney can determine if they are reasonable or not.

If you have a situation where an employee comes to you indicating that he is injured and suggests or infers in any manner that it is work-related, your obligation is to immediately provide to him a workers' compensation claim form. It does not matter if you are convinced that he is a fraud or a sham. Rather, under most jurisdictions you have an automatic obligation to provide such documentation to an employee, regardless of the merit of his claim.

In many jurisdictions your failure to provide such a claim constitutes grounds for civil penalties. It would be a mistake to make any derogatory or negative comments to such employees when they submit even what appear to be obviously fraudulent claims. The realities are that they can use your words against you for retaliation claims. More specifically, if you later do have to terminate this employee, he can always come back and assert that the real reason you are terminating him is because you perceived that his prior workers' compensation claim was a fraud and a sham and now you are retaliating against him by terminating his employment.

Remember retaliation claims (see Section 12.0) can be quite expensive. You do have the right, on the other hand, to notify your workers' compensation carrier that you believe the claim is fraudulent. On many occasions, at the direction of many of my clients, I have sent a detailed letter to the workers' compensation carrier raising the fact that this matter is fraudulent and should not be settled, and pointing out to the workers' compensation carrier their statutory obligations to conduct good-faith investigations instead of charging my client unnecessary increased premiums.

Over the years, in several instances where an employee has asserted they were unable to work or even drive or walk, I have had clients who have taken photographs or videos of such individuals that have been utilized by workers' compensation carriers to pursue these fraudulent claimants. Obviously in taking such extraordinary actions, the boss or supervisor must be careful not to in any manner violate the right of privacy of the employee, but rather can only take such photographs in areas where the employee does not have any reasonable expectation of privacy. Examples of areas where employees do not have a reasonable expectation of privacy are pretty much any area where the employer provides to them notification that they may be subjected to photographs or videotaping by specifying such in the employer's employee manual. Also employers oftentimes post signs in particular areas in the workplace indicating that the employees may be videotaped. Further pretty much anywhere a person can be viewed by another person (with the exception of a restroom) would be an area that could be under surveillance; and an employee would not have a reasonable expectation of right of privacy unless, for whatever reason, the employer has created some expectation of right of privacy. Examples of such situations, besides bathrooms, might be separate lockers or dressing rooms, as well as under some circumstances, some employers provide places for their employees to meditate or pray, etc.

Insomnia, according to doctors, is the number-one health-care complaint in America.

*Based on statistical documentation,
the jobs of logger, pilot, asbestos worker,
metal worker, and electrician are the most dangerous.*

Section 5.3: Handling Excessive Absenteeism

Your first concern should be the reason for the absenteeism. There now exists a whole host of state, federal, and foreign laws allowing employees to be absent (typically without pay) for a variety of reasons, while at the same time requiring that the employer keep that employee's position available for the employee when the employee returns. Such absenteeism includes absenteeism for medical and disability leaves, pregnancy leave, military leave, family leave, absence over certain activities involving the employee's children including school activities and functions, etc. Depending upon the state, some of these laws apply to employers with as few as one employee, while others apply to employers who have twenty-five or more employees and in some instances fifty or more employees.

At the same time, the laws recognize the fact that employers cannot continue to operate and do business without employees. As a result, the solution provided is to allow employers to retain temporary employees to handle such jobs and responsibilities during the "regular" employee's absence. The realities of course faced by bosses and supervisors include the fact that often these absences can be for weeks, months, or in some instances in excess of a year or longer. It is difficult to recruit temporary employees based on such vague time parameters.

The response by the state, federal, and foreign governments to such employer concerns has been in essence "adjust." The burden to "adjust" usually applies to those situations wherein the employee has a temporary disability preventing her from doing her normal job duties and responsibilities, even with reasonable accommodation. If that disability becomes permanent, and the employee is unable to perform the job duties and responsibilities even with reasonable accommodation(s), then the employer is no longer obligated to allow the employee to have a leave of absence and is justified in ceasing the employment relationship.

Once again this is a fairly complicated area involving not only issues dealing with the *Americans with Disabilities Act* (in the United States), but also dealing with the obligation to not discriminate against individuals with handicaps and certain medical conditions, and therefore it's a good idea to consult with a qualified attorney.

As always, ask yourself in looking at the particular situation whether or not a "Blue-Haired Lady" (see Step #2) is going to side with you in a lawsuit, or the employee who is sitting next to you in the courtroom. It has been my experience that juries are pretty sympathetic toward individuals who are disabled or handicapped, and accordingly that is why those classifications of lawsuits are pretty popular with employee's attorneys. Consequently, you had better have some overwhelming justification as to why it was you could not allow such a person a leave of absence to take care of her problem, as opposed to firing her.

The law is clear on the other hand that employers have the right to terminate employees who are absent for no protected reason. It is less clear about dealing with those employees who fail to comply with the employer's policies and procedures requiring giving reasonable notice about such absences and/or maintaining updated leave of absence authorizations from the employee's qualified physician. Accordingly, make sure your personnel handbook has a detailed policy relating to the employee's obligations and duties relating to leaves of absence and providing notification and updated release documentation, and always consult legal counsel before firing a disabled employee who fails to fill out the proper forms.

One of the most common questions asked of lawyers by bosses and supervisors is, "How long do I have to allow an employee to continue on workers' compensation before I fire him?" The lawyer's response typically is, "What reason, if any, do you as a boss or supervisor have as to why you cannot replace that employee with a temporary employee and allow your prior employee to remain on workers' compensation leave?" If your answer is simply that you don't want him to continue receiving health insurance benefits (which is typically the answer given), you can pretty well guess that a "Blue-Haired Lady" is not going to be particularly sympathetic to your response.

Frequently, when employees perceive that they are about to be terminated, they will file workers' compensation claims in order to maintain their health insurance benefits, and also in order to prevent their being fired. If you do fire any employees shortly after they file a workers' compensation claim, it may appear that you were motivated to do such because of their claim, which is against the law.

So long as an employee is complying with your policies and procedures relating to keeping you updated with notification from her physician about her anticipated date of return, in compliance with your policies, it is advisable not to discipline her. Most of the time in these circumstances, the employer has not previously documented any performance problems; but now while the employee is off on some type of protected leave of absence, the employer is attempting to claim that she was performing poorly prior to the protected leave of absence. Most "Blue-Haired Ladies" view this as unlikely and more of a form of retaliation by the employer against the employee for taking the protected leave of absence.

Such is another reason why it is important for bosses and supervisors to, in a timely manner, maintain and document deficiencies regarding their employees. If it appears that an employee is going to milk the system and your health care benefits for what you consider to be an inordinate amount of time, you should consult an attorney.

Another question that frequently arises is how long must an employer maintain health insurance benefits for employees who are on such protected leaves of absence? State and federal laws (and some foreign laws) are somewhat in conformity that typically if the leave of absence is because of a work-related injury, the employee is entitled to greater protection than if the injury is not work related.

As a general rule, it's not advisable to have a flat rule (as some employers have attempted) wherein they cap the benefits at six months after the individual has gone on any type of leave of absence. Leaves of absence can vary significantly, whether they are because of medical conditions, disabilities, pregnancies, etc.; and therefore, that needs to be taken into consideration regarding how long an employer provides benefits in each case.

From a legal standpoint, the safest methodology to deal with such individuals is to have a policy of getting them back to work as soon as reasonably possible by providing reasonable accommodations to the employees to get them back on to the job. If the employee involved is someone who simply wants health insurance benefits for his family without actually working, this back-to-work approach usually gets him off the dime so that he either returns back to work and becomes productive, or he quits.

As it relates to those employees who are malingerers, most experts agree that getting them back to work is frequently the best approach. Keep in mind that if they return to work doing lesser job duties and responsibilities, you as a boss or supervisor can decrease their pay to what other employees who are doing the same duties and responsibilities are receiving.

As to those employees who pay a portion of their own health care insurance benefits, make sure you have a policy in your employee handbook that addresses such situations. Usually the language will specify that an employee's obligation for his or her health care benefits continues during any leave of absence he or she has for any purpose and will not be advanced by the employer. Accordingly the manual will specify that if the employee fails to pay for such health care benefits, then the insurance carrier will cancel his or her insurance. It is advisable, however, that before any health insurance policy is canceled, that the boss or supervisor notify the employee directly of the fact that it is going to be canceled before it is actually canceled because of the employee's failure to contribute or pay for the insurance premiums, and to document that as well by a confirming letter to the employee confirming the telephone call. Remember, an employer does not have an obligation to subsidize an employee's contributions for health care insurance unless the employer assumes that obligation, which is a precedent that most bosses and supervisors would want to avoid.

Lastly, as to those employees who are absent without any type of notification whatsoever, make sure you have in your personnel handbook a written policy confirming the fact that if they are absent for three or more days, that they will be deemed to have abandoned their job.

Each year, allergies cause Americans to miss more than
3,000,000 days of work.

Section 5.4: Handling Habitually Late Employees

Get rid of them. Once you start allowing one employee to get away with violations of your policies and procedures, the other employees will feel that they have a right to do the same. It is the employees' obligation to work under your schedule, not vice versa. Once you start allowing employees to dictate when they will and will not come to work, they then feel that they are irreplaceable and you cannot do without them, and the situation will continue to grow worse and worse. For employees to argue they didn't really understand that they were to get to work on time either means that they think you're stupid or they are stupid. Either way, these are not the type of people you want to continue working for you.

Give reasonable warnings and then go to termination. Do not engage in a pattern of making repeated empty threats. A reasonable approach would be after a few verbal warnings, within a reasonable time frame, to provide to the employee a memorandum reminding him that he is at will; however, any further violations of the company's policy by being late without authorization within the next six months will result in termination of employment. Then if he is late again within that time frame, terminate his employment by following the recommendations set forth in Section 10.0 et seq. herein.

Many excuses are given by employees for being tardy.
The top 5 are as follows:
1) Traffic
2) Oversleeping
3) Procrastination
4) Household chores
5) Car problems

Section 5.5: Handling Employees Whom You Suspect of Organizing Union Activities

The bottom line here is, let them! State and federal laws (and many foreign laws) make it very clear that you do not have a right to in any manner interfere with any union organizing activities other than those that are occurring during working hours in your place of business (unless you have waived that right). One of the ways in which you might waive that right, according to specific cases, is that you allow employees and other companies to come in and put announcements up on your bulletin boards and/or sell other products such as Avon or Mary Kay Cosmetics, etc. It is for this reason that most knowledgeable employers have written personnel policies that preclude employees or anyone from coming in and selling anything on their premises. They do this, not because they are against cosmetics, but rather because they don't want to open the door so as to allow union representatives to come in and start organizing during working hours in their facilities. The law precludes employers from discriminating against unions in this regard.

As a general rule, however, employees have very few limitations imposed upon them to prevent them from union organizing activities.

Union organizing activities involve, in general, a specified number of employees indicating or signing documentation that they want to become a union. Therefore, the matter is typically put to a vote by the group of employees involved. The employer does have a right (during what is called the campaign period) before the election to campaign as well. Limitations, however, are imposed on both the union organizers, as well as the employer, not to engage in certain conduct, which has been more commonly referred to under the acronym of S. P. I. T. This means employers cannot conduct *Surveillance*, make *Promises*, *Interrogate* or *Threaten* employees in any manner. The penalties can be enormous against not only bosses, but also supervisors. This is again an area wherein you would want to consult with a qualified attorney.

REMEMBER, THE BEST ADVOCATE FOR A UNION COMING INTO YOUR PLACE OF BUSINESS IS YOU! Employees do not normally go out and seek to become unionized. Most recognize and understand that a part of the compensation they are currently receiving will have to be paid to a union; and therefore, economically, becoming unionized generally makes no sense. That is unless a majority of the employees involved are convinced that they are being so mistreated that it is well worth it for them to pay money out of their pocket to a union so as to require the employer to become more fair and reasonable.

THE MOTHER OF UNION
ORGANIZATION IN THE UNITED STATES

Mary Harris, who was known as "Mother Jones," was a schoolteacher in Michigan in the 1850s. In 1861, after marrying George Jones, she moved to Chicago and operated a dressmaking operation that perished during the Chicago fire of 1871. Thereafter, she got involved with U.S. labor and traveled all over the country organizing workers in the coal mines and garment, railroad, and steel industries for over fifty years up until her death where she was 100 years of age.

Section 5.6: Handling Issues Regarding Employees' Rights of Privacy

Keep in mind, while looking through this section, that both the employer and the supervisors are personally liable if you violate an employee's right of privacy. If such occurs, you are liable for all the same types of damages as for wrongful termination or discrimination (see Section 1.0 through 1.7) with the caveat that it will be somewhat more difficult for the employee to recover attorney's fees.

Section 5.6(a): Written Policies and Procedures

In your personnel handbook, it is important to include detailed and specific polices and procedures regarding the fact that all personnel and medical information about employees are to be treated confidentially. It is important for you as a boss or supervisor to have established that the company actively and aggressively protects the right of privacy of your employees. Further, that any violation will not be tolerated. Traditionally, in personnel handbooks, this is one of the more detailed sections.

"What you cannot enforce, do not command."
—Socrates

Section 5.6(b): Surveillance

There has been a significant amount of publicity relating to the employer's right to conduct surveillance of its employees. The law generally is that employers have a right to conduct surveillance of their employees (including by use of video cameras, with the exception of any union organizing activities as set forth in Section 5.4). In general, the employer has a right to conduct surveillance of its employees in any area wherein the employee does not have a legitimate expectation of a right of privacy. This includes basically any and all areas wherein the employer has made it clear (typically through written policies) that the employee does not have an expectation of right of privacy, such as common work areas, desks, common hallways, etc. This does not include areas where "Blue-Haired Ladies" would perceive that the employee had a legitimate belief that they were not being watched. Examples of such include attempts by employers to videotape their employees by way of an invisible camera over the sink in a washroom or any type of surveillance in a bathroom.

Section 5.6(c): Searches and Seizures

The law here is similar to surveillance, in that generally an employer has a right to conduct searches and seizures so long as such does not involve any search or seizure of an area where the employee has a legitimate expectation of right of privacy. Once again, the best way to address this is through the employer's personnel handbook, wherein the employer has specified in detail that the employees do not have an expectation of right of privacy. Normally this relates to anything contained on or in the employees' computers, voicemail, email, or anything in their desks or lockers or any other location on company premises. While such a policy will not allow the boss or supervisor to conduct body cavity searches, it will go a long way to broadening the employer's rights. Also included with these types of policies are the standard policies that specify that all work products or anything else created by the employees on computers, etc. during working hours or at the employer's place of business, or on behalf of the employer, belongs to the employer.

Some may believe that having a policy regarding eliminating the employee's expectation of privacy is inconsistent with the general philosophy of this book (i.e., to treat employees with dignity and *respect*), which to some degree is true. However, there have been significant abuses by employees relating to information maintained on their computers, as well as bringing paraphernalia and inappropriate items to the place of business, including weapons and drugs, which necessitate the adoption of such a practice. In most cases, employees understand this approach, so long as it is applied consistently.

Researchers say one in four people admit
to snooping in their host's medicine cabinet.

Section 5.6(d): Polygraph Tests

While an employer has a right, with the employee's consent, to use polygraph tests, the employer should never do such. More specifically, if the employee refuses to take part in the polygraph examination, said employee has just pretty much guaranteed himself a lifetime job with you. The reason for this is that employees in such a circumstance can take the position that any disciplinary action, including termination, taken toward him after his refusal to agree to a polygraph is not for performance reasons, but rather is in retaliation for his refusal to participate in the polygraph test. Such retaliation is prohibited by state, federal, and some foreign laws and constitutes a violation of public policy, subjecting not only the bosses but also the supervisors to personal liability, as is more specifically set forth in Sections 1.1 through 1.6 herein.

The brain can record about eighty-six million bits
of information each day.

Section 5.6(e): Drug Testing (see Section 4.7 herein regarding Pre-Employment Testing)

Section 5.7: Handling the Media (see Section 10.4 regarding media)

Section 6.0

Sexual Harassment

*"Men and women are a lot alike in certain situations.
Like when they're both on fire, they're exactly alike."*
—Dave Attell

Section 6.1: Handling Sexual Harassment Matters

The area of sexual harassment continues to be one of the most misunderstood and vigorously litigated areas in employment law. Some of the more common misunderstandings are as follows:

- The perception of bosses and supervisors that in order for them to have any liability about such, that it must have occurred in the workplace, during working hours, wherein the employee has made a formal complaint about such.

- That typically the inappropriate conduct engaged in must have been directed toward the person who has made the complaint.

- If the person who is now making the complaint previously consented to similar conduct, that there is no sexual harassment.

While wrongful termination and employment discrimination lawsuits are some of the most emotional lawsuits that exist, the subcategory of sexual harassment is the most explosive of all such claims. Typically if the person who is making the claim does not prevail, she will be viewed as either a prude or a gold digging low-life that cannot be trusted. Even if she does prevail, she will typically be viewed as someone who cannot be trusted in any future workplace.

As it relates to the individual whom the claim is brought against, no matter how much an employer promises to keep such confidential, the realities are that something will be leaked. This will, under all circumstances, make it very difficult for this person to ever get a job again. If she in fact goes through a publicized litigation, her chances of getting another comparable job in the same geographic area are about as likely as a frog growing wings.

Section 6.2: What Is Sexual Harassment?

Sexual harassment in employment typically consists of conduct or activities, wherein one individual, regardless of sex, engages in nonconsensual inappropriate conduct toward the victim because of her sex, which has the effect of altering, changing, or interfering with the victim's job. Examples of such harassment has been defined as broadly as leering, wherein one person in essence looks up and down the body of the victim. Traditionally sexual harassment has been applied in the Landlord/Tenant and Employer/Employee relationships; however, it has now been broadened substantially beyond those limitations. For the purposes of this book, we will not go into all of those other situations. The realities are that if sexual harassment is defined as leering, then I would suggest that sexual harassment most likely occurs in every working environment on at least a weekly, if not daily basis (particularly where there are opposite sexes; however, keep in mind that sexual harassment can occur between individuals of the same sex).

Once again, the issue here is not whether or not the sexual harassment occurred, but rather what's the value (see Section 3.0). Most "Blue-Haired Ladies" do not get terribly upset about a leer, and therefore most plaintiffs' attorneys will not take these types of cases on a contingency fee basis. On the other hand, if there is some type of physical touching, or if the employee actually complained about the conduct and was retaliated against by her supervisor or boss, or if the sexual harassment is actually engaged in toward the employee by her supervisor, then the value of the case goes up astronomically. Frequently these can go into the seven-digit number range.

Before filing a sexual harassment lawsuit, in many states there is no requirement that an employee actually objects to the conduct. The failure of the alleged victim to complain about the conduct, however, is admissible to the jury, which they will evaluate to determine whether or not the alleged victim is actually telling the truth. The explanation usually provided by most alleged victims is that they did not complain because in the past they saw that the company did nothing regarding such situations. Such employees often also claim that the person to whom they were supposed to complain was actually the person doing the harassing, or that they were simply too afraid to complain because of the possibilities of retaliation or physical harm.

Keep in mind, however, that it does not take much for sexual harassment to occur, including another employee simply overhearing a dirty joke being told in the workplace. Under these circumstances, not only is the individual who tells the jokes liable for sexual harassment, but also depending upon the circumstances, so also might the supervisor as well as the employer. This is especially true if the boss or supervisor knew or should have known about such joke telling and took no reasonable action, or if the person who is doing the joke telling is the supervisor or boss.

"We have got an awful lot of members
who don't understand that harass is one word, not two."
—Rep. Pat Schroeder

Section 6.3: Defenses To Sexual Harassment Claims

The typical defenses are as follows:

(1) It did not occur.
(2) It was consensual.
(3) Statute of Limitations (typically between one and two years in most jurisdictions).
(4) That the alleged victim did not follow the company's policies and procedures regarding reporting the complaint.
(5) That the person engaging in the sexual harassment was not working in the course and scope of his employment at the time involved, and therefore the employer is not responsible for such.

THE REALITIES ARE THAT USUALLY IT GETS DOWN TO WHOM THE "BLUE-HAIRED LADY" BELIEVES.

As to the defense of consent, once again, that's simply a credibility battle. As it relates to the defense of the statute of limitations, such are pretty long; and therefore, most of these claims are brought within the applicable time frames. As to the defense regarding following the employer's policies and procedures, it is very helpful for employers these days to have detailed policies and procedures in their handbook about the requirement of employees to report sexual harassment. There are some cases that indicate that if an employee fails to report such in compliance with the company's policies and procedures (and if there is no material change in the alleged victim's working conditions, such as loss of wages, demotion, discipline or termination), then the employer may not be liable for the actions of its sexually harassing employees.

Realistically, if a supervisor goes out to the local bar after work for a beer with his subordinate and comes on to her, although outside of the workplace, not only is the supervisor personally liable for sexual harassment, but quite frequently so will the employer.

"When a stupid man is doing something he is ashamed of,
he always declares that it is his duty."
—George Bernard Shaw

Section 6.4: Investigating Sexual Harassment

How investigations are conducted can vary dramatically depending upon each and every situation involved. As a general rule, your place of business should have a person designated to whom all such complaints are made. If, for whatever reason the complaint is against that person, your policies and procedures should have an alternate person (who is senior to the alleged harasser) who is available to receive such claims.

Besides making sure that the persons who are doing the investigation are knowledgeable, also make sure that any time you are talking with witnesses, have at least two persons present, preferably one of each sex. Make sure at all times the investigation is conducted confidentially, and make sure that you tell all witnesses to whom you speak that the matter is not to be discussed in the workplace during working hours. Further, after initially talking with each of the witnesses involved, have them write up a summary of what information they have that is relevant to the particular issue. Also make sure that you ask each of the witnesses the name or names of any and all other individuals they think are relevant regarding your investigation. Conduct the investigation impartially and within a reasonable time frame, while utilizing advice of counsel (see Step #21).

Never tell anyone that you will keep the investigation confidential. In order to do an objective investigation, it may well be necessary for you to disclose the name of the individual providing the information to others. The claimant may have some bias or prejudice that you need to consider before making a determination as to whether or not the sexual harassment occurred. On the other hand, do tell all persons to whom you speak that are witnesses in the matter that you will keep such as confidential as is reasonably possible under the circumstances.

The realities in conducting a sexual harassment investigation are that, for the most part, they involve situations wherein only two witnesses have knowledge about what occurred. Typically these two are the alleged victim and the alleged harasser. Rarely, if ever, does the alleged harasser come out and state, "I admit I am a sexual harasser." In most instances, you typically have two fairly credible witnesses whose stories are 180 degrees apart.

Your job, if you are the person designated to investigate the matter, is to determine which of the two is more credible. The law does not require that you be right in this regard, but it does require that you conduct a reasonable investigation; and therefore you are going to want to be able to demonstrate that at all times you were thorough, detailed, and objective in your investigation. The burden is going to be placed upon you if this matter goes to litigation to establish specifically why you believe one person versus the other. In many instances, this is not possible; and therefore the person who is investigating the matter may determine there was insufficient evidence to make a decision. If it's of any assistance, again pretend that a "Blue-Haired Lady" is sitting down next to you while the investigation is being conducted; and based on the information provided, what do you think she would have decided?

Section 6.5: Appropriate Discipline in a Sexual Harassment Matter

In this, like all other employment situations, the law requires that if the employer has determined some type of inappropriate or improper conduct occurred, YOU MUST TAKE SUCH ACTION WHICH A "BLUE-HAIRED LADY" WOULD BELIEVE WOULD HAVE RESULTED IN THE CESSATION OF SUCH INAPPROPRIATE CONDUCT.

In some instances, however, the employees are not entitled to a second shot. Some of the more easy examples of these include assault, battery, being under the influence on the job, etc. Because sexual harassment can vary anywhere from making an off-color remark to a sexual assault and battery, the discipline necessarily has to fit the crime. Keep in mind, however, that if you have determined that sexual harassment did in fact occur, and if you are not going to terminate the alleged harasser's employment, then you have been put on notice of his or her conduct. If such occurs again with that same employee, you will most likely be living out of Motel 6. Therefore, you have a significant incentive to make the right call.

Also keep in mind that the alleged victim does not simply have to accept whatever determination you make. She may well take the position that because of your lack of fortitude in addressing the situation, she was constructively discharged and sue you, not only for constructive discharge, but also for ratifying the acts of the sexual harasser. This will subject you to the same type of damages as are set forth in Sections 1.1 through 1.6 herein.

Section 7.0

Handling Violence in the Workplace

Incidents of violence in the workplace are increasing at an ever-alarming rate. Besides having a written policy in your personnel handbook about how to deal with such, be alert to some of the warning signs. Remember, you may be all that stands between someone (including yourself) from being harmed or even worse. Therefore, this is an area wherein being alert is justified not only morally, but also legally. You want to create a working atmosphere wherein everyone understands that this is no joking matter.

Your policy should be that anyone who makes threats of violence or harm to anyone will promptly and severely be dealt with. Many states and foreign countries now have laws that allow and sometimes require employers to obtain restraining orders to restrain individuals from coming into contact with their employees under specific circumstances. Again, the defense of advice of counsel (see Step #21) applies in these situations and further invokes the "Blue-Haired Lady" doctrine in determining whether or not the circumstances justify taking action.

If you've got a situation, for instance, wherein you're going to terminate an employee's employment, and you have concerns about the potential for violence, it's not particularly expensive to retain the services of a reputable security company (as opposed to Barney Fife, Inc.). Have one of their qualified employees present in the next room, in case something goes wrong. Make prearrangements with your security guard that he is to come into the room when you provide some type of code. When I have made such arrangements, my code was when I yelled the word, "Help!"

It's far better to invest $200 to $300 for a security guard in what hopefully are rare instances, as opposed to the alternative.

There are of course many warning signals regarding when problems might arise, including the following:

(1) Prior history of actual violent or abusive conduct by the individual involved

(2) Any history of abuse and/or improper use of drugs or alcohol

(3) Individuals who appear to be loners and have difficulties in social interactions and/or relations, etc.

(4) Individuals who are not only familiar with but appear to have an extreme interest in weaponry of any kind

(5) Individuals whose lives appear emotionally dependent on who they are in their job

(6) Individuals suffering from depression or erratic mood changes, etc. (A swastika tattooed on the forehead might be a hint.)

If you have to terminate an individual fitting this type of profile, in addition to following the procedure set forth in Section 10.0 hereinafter, and having security available, make special arrangements to have more than one person present when it comes time for him to remove his personal effects. If either prior to or during the termination, the person actually becomes threatening, do not hesitate to contact the legal authorities and/or obtain a restraining order. You might want to consider beefing up security around your workplace and your home if necessary.

Without sounding too paranoid, learning self-defense is always a good idea; and further, many jurisdictions allow individuals to possess mace and similar deterrents. In practicing for over twenty-five years, and representing literally thousands of clients, I have been involved in only a few instances of violence in workplace situations, none of which resulted in serious physical injury.

Therefore I do not want to over-dramatize the likelihood of this occurring; however, it is better to be safe than sorry.

Surveys have shown that one in six employees
during their employment have become so mad
at another worker within the last year
and felt like punching them,
but did not actually follow through.

Section 8.0

Handling Existing Unlawful/Improper Employment Practices

Section 8.1: Wage and Hour Violations

What do you do when you find out that for the last four years, you have not been properly paying overtime to your employees? Perhaps you have misclassified your employees and not given them any overtime whatsoever because you thought that they were exempt, whereas in reality, they were not.

What do you do when you find out that you have misclassified an employee for the last several years, and that in reality, the workers' compensation rate you owe on the employee is substantially higher than what you have been paying?

What do you do when you find out that the frequency which you pay your employees is out of compliance with state, federal, and foreign law in that the time periods within which you are paying your employees is in violation of applicable law, and has been so for the last five years?

What do you do when you find out that for the last several years, one of your employees has been falsifying records resulting in false information being provided to either customers or even the government?

What do you do when you find out the company for whom you work has been violating some other state, federal, or foreign law for the last several years, such as unlawfully employing illegal immigrants, etc.?

To answer these questions for most supervisors is not that difficult. In these instances, your best defense is to immediately report to your supervisor once you have learned of such information so as to make it clear that you were not in any manner withholding or taking part in any such unlawful action. Some supervisors, so as to make sure there is no ambiguity about such, document reporting such matters to their higher ups. In many instances, supervisors have concerns or fears about potential retaliation and simply keep a diary of the incidents. As a supervisor (assuming you are not the party who initiated such but simply found out about the matter), your best defense again is to not let this sit on your desk, but rather to make sure that you have reported it to a higher up so they can take the responsibility.

The theory on this approach is that once the people in power become aware of whatever the matter is, they will immediately act; otherwise they face personal liability. Consequently, if you are a mid-level manager or supervisor wherein you may not have the ability to control or deal with the situation yourself, you do have the ability to report such, which is what you should do.

If you are the party who actually engaged in the unlawful or inappropriate actions, you should probably consult with your own legal counsel. In most of these instances, it still makes sense that you would report such to your supervisor. Otherwise not only have you engaged in such conduct inappropriately, but also your failure to disclose such facts and information may constitute additional grounds or claims against you personally.

What if, however, you are the boss? In essence, you are the person where "the buck stops." From an ethical standpoint as well as a moralistic standpoint, it is inappropriate and improper for an attorney to recommend that his client engage in any type of unlawful conduct. Accordingly, when clients come to me with such situations, I cannot under any circumstances recommend that they engage in unlawful conduct.

If the circumstances or situation involves criminal conduct, there are additional obligations imposed upon an attorney ethically as well as legally. In most non-criminal situations, my approach is to simply advise my clients of their options, and they will in turn make the decision as to which approach they will take.

If the violation, as is frequently the case, involves failure to comply with civil laws regarding wage and hour claims, the boss will typically have one of the following options:

(1) Go back and make all of the harmed employees whole by not only providing back to them all of the wages to which they are entitled, along with the penalties, but also addressing all of the loss of benefits, etc. that they would have been entitled to, such as failure to pay all of the applicable social security, FICA, etc. for the entire time frame that is involved.

(2) The boss can elect to pay a portion of what arguably might be owed in the hope that this will resolve the matter. However, understandably with this approach, there may continue to be liability and exposure because once the employer becomes aware of the violation of such laws, his failure to address such fully, now strongly supports a claim for intentional misconduct, which involves even greater penalties.

(3) The boss may elect to pay out only a portion of the potential claims, under the theory that there may well be legitimate defenses to such; and therefore only a portion is being paid out with the understanding that he may be subject to liability.

(4) The boss may simply elect to take a risk and hope that no one finds out about whatever the situation is and not pay back any of the funds. However, the boss would usually, effective immediately, correct his practices so as to bring him in compliance with applicable law. This option, of course, involves substantially more risk and liability.

(5) Another option is that the employer decides that not only is he not going to pay anything for past violations, but rather he is going to keep on with his practices, which of course involves even greater liability and pays for my kids' college education.

There are legitimate legal arguments justifying an employer not to go back and make employees whole for prior employer transgressions, such as the statute of limitations. In many states, the applicable statute of limitations for violation of wage and hour claims runs between three to four years; and therefore there is an argument that if an employer violated wage and hour claims before that time period, legally they are not required to pay back those funds. Therefore these options are obviously worth considering, which is why it is strongly recommended that if you as a boss become aware of unlawful actions that your company has been involved with, you do immediately consult with legal counsel so as to determine the various options and their consequences.

Another common issue that arises under wage and hour violations is the situation where employees have been classified as exempt; however, now the employer has determined that the employees should have been classified as non-exempt. The issue arises as to how an employer handles that situation.

Once again in this matter, there are several options, including advising the employees they were simply misclassified and going back and paying them for all amounts previously owed and making them whole. Another option is to do such only for the applicable statute of limitations involved. Another approach some employers take is to simply assume the risk and not necessarily pay everything that is owed, or at a minimum take the position that there are legal arguments to contest all such claims, and take the risk that they are right.

Another approach frequently taken by employers is that it is really unclear as to the classification because this is one of those situations in the gray area; and so to be on the safe side, they simply convert the employees over to non-exempt status so as to avoid such ambiguities and also to make sure that the employees are given the benefit of the doubt. Of course once this is done, employees are going to wonder why it is that they have been converted to non-exempt versus exempt. Therefore, make sure that you have as good an idea as possible as to whether or not you really are in the gray zone versus the red zone wherein it is clearly obvious that you were in violation of law, and accordingly would be subject to penalties, etc.

Section 8.2: Converting to At-Will Employment from For-Cause Employment

Quite frequently, employers advise me that they do not have employee handbooks, manuals, or employment applications making any reference to at-will employment. They indicate that they really never even knew of that term and now want to convert all of their employees to at-will employees as opposed to for-cause employees (see Step #14).

As referenced in Step #14, most jurisdictions in the United States assume that employees are at will unless it has been waived. Consequently, even if you are a boss or supervisor of a company that has never, ever even utilized the term "at-will employment," it may well still be that your employees are still deemed at will. Assuming that to be the case, you really are not converting from for-cause status to at-will status, but rather simply clarifying that relationship by including such into your employee handbooks as well as your applications.

If it is abundantly clear that for whatever reason, your company has treated its employees as for-cause employees and waived the doctrine of at-will employment, you still have the option of taking the approach that you are simply changing the employment relationship. Under this approach, greater liability of course exists for the boss or supervisor, and therefore it would be advisable to consult with legal counsel.

The general approach is that if the employees want to continue working with you, it is now your position that they are at will; and if they accept that arrangement, then you would argue that they have waived their "for-cause status." This approach gets a little more complicated and can be tricky and again should only be done under advice of legal counsel.

Section 9.0

Setting Up the Business Properly for Employment Purposes

There are obviously a number of considerations in setting up a business and the effects that it will have not only upon bosses but also the supervisors. There are of course tax considerations and a variety of other factors, including corporation issues of which the author is not really qualified to comment upon. Suffice it to say that in the employment arena, it is frequently advantageous for the owner of such business to have a valid corporate structure that has the additional benefit of insulating the individual from personal liability for the acts of others in the employment arena.

Accordingly, as with regard to setting up any business, again it is fundamental that consultation with competent legal counsel is advisable in not only setting up the structure of the place of employment, but also making sure that at all times the employer is in compliance with applicable state, federal, and foreign laws. This includes in addition having proper employment applications (see Step #3), maintaining proper written policies (see Step #10), and having supervisors and managers subjected to proper training and education (see Step #12). This would of course also involve making sure that you have obtained all insurance you deem applicable (see Step #23), and of course read this book.

Section 10.0

Handling the Termination of an Employee

As Mark Twain once stated, "I cannot help but notice that there is no problem between us that cannot be solved by your departure." Terminating an employee's employment is and should be the very last resort (see Step #7). However, if everything else has failed, and this is all that is left, then the manner in which you handle the termination is crucial.

"Failure is the opportunity to begin again, more intelligently."
—Henry Ford

Section 10.1: Proper Warning

Make sure that you've done everything reasonably possible so as to make certain that in most situations, no terminations are going to be a surprise to your employees. That means that you've given them all prior warning notices, etc. Therefore this should not, under any circumstances, be a shock to them. Remember if your employees are surprised when they are fired, it is either because they are stupid or because you didn't do your job by letting them know on a consistent and continual basis about their deficiencies. Usually it is the latter. This of course includes making sure that you have an adequate paper trail regarding your concerns.

Surveys show that on average in the United States, eighty percent of employees will be fired at least once.

Section 10.2: Arranging the Logistics

The "Do's" when terminating an employee:

(1)   Whenever possible, termination should occur at the end of the day so as to prevent the employee from having to go through the embarrassment of facing other employees.

(2)   It's helpful to typically schedule such matters for weekdays other than Fridays, so she and her family will not be brooding over the weekend and watching attorney commercials.

(3)   Shortly before the termination is to occur, make sure the accounting department has been notified to prepare the final check and has also been advised to keep all of this confidential. There is nothing worse than an employee hearing that she is being fired through a file clerk.

(4)   Make sure that a confidential room is available and you have another person who is senior to the person to be terminated who will be present during the termination itself.

(5)   If you believe the circumstances justify such, make sure that you've consulted with legal counsel in all aspects about the termination, in advance of the termination itself (see Step #21).

(6)   You'll also want to make sure that you have available at the time of the termination all the necessary documentation, including the exit interview form (see Step #5), all Cobra documentation and any other materials or documents that need to be signed by the employee or provided to the employee at the time of termination.

(7)   It is also helpful to have a general outline of what it is you are going to say that you have reviewed before the termination.

(8)   In some instances, it may be justified to provide to the employee a memorandum confirming what is said during the

termination (typically you'll only want to do this where you're concerned that the individual is going to pursue some type of litigation and you want some type of confirming documentation to go to him and therefore his attorney outlining what has happened). Such memorandums typically remind the employee that he is an at-will employee and also remind him of the areas of at least some [i.e., including but not limited to] concern, which hopefully you have already discussed with him previously.

(9) If this is a situation wherein you are going to make an offer of severance pay (see Step #9), make sure that you have in advance of the meeting all the necessary release documents prepared, including the severance check.

(10) Keep in mind that in everything that you do regarding the termination, you want to be as reasonable as possible (see Steps #1, 2, and 16). Keep the physical setting itself as non-confrontational as possible. This is typically why many bosses and supervisors prefer round conference room tables to sitting across the desk during such situations.

(11) To keep the intimidation factor to a minimum, make sure that there are no more than two persons who are providing notification to the employee.

(12) Because terminations can become quite emotional, always have tissues and water available.

(13) Finally, also make sure that if the employee involved has access to computers, etc., that you have made the appropriate arrangements so as to prevent them from erasing and/or changing any information on your system and/or removing any information.

> *Studies show that when it comes to smiling,*
> *women do so more frequently*
> *when giving bad news than do men.*

Section 10.3: The Termination Itself

Throughout this process (besides keeping this non-confrontational), you want to treat the employee with as much respect as is reasonably possible. The discussion itself should be to the point, but courteous and professional at all times. Make sure that in getting the employee to the meeting that such is done in a diplomatic and confidential fashion.

Years ago I defended a situation wherein literally dozens of employees were terminated. In that matter, the employer literally had everyone summoned separately to a specific room over a loudspeaker, one by one. By the second employee, everyone knew that everyone thereafter was being fired, and it was very much like the march of death.

Accordingly, make sure that you have made arrangements for the employee to meet with you at a particular time at the end of the day. This usually has the added benefit of putting him on notice that something is about to happen, so he can somewhat get himself adjusted both mentally and emotionally. However, do not give this notice more than twenty to thirty minutes in advance, if practicable. When the individual arrives for the meeting, make sure that you and the other person who is present on behalf of the employer understands her role, which is primarily to be there as a witness and nothing more. The person who does most of the talking should be the person for whom the employee has the greatest respect.

In these situations, I typically recommend to my clients that they state essentially the following, after the initial salutations:

> "Unfortunately, and as you may have assumed, it is time for our company and yourself to come to a parting of the ways. We would, however, like to have your input as how to best accomplish this. More specifically, if you prefer, we can immediately accept your resignation; or if you would rather, we can terminate your employment effective immediately. Which would you like to do?"

It has been my experience, having gone through many of these, that when explained in this way, they are much more likely to request that they be allowed to resign. If during the discussions, the employee wants to argue or debate with you the merits of the termination, simply advise the individual that that decision has already been made and there is nothing constructive that will come out of further discussing the matter. Do not allow yourself to become involved in such a discussion under any circumstances, in that usually nothing beneficial will come from these communications for you, the boss or supervisor.

In most instances, employees will tell you that they want to think the matter over and get back to you. However, do not vary from your position. The option of allowing them to resign is a courtesy you are providing to them if they want it. However, if they do not, simply go ahead and terminate them effective immediately. Do tell them this before you terminate them because they may want a second chance to decide.

Are you in effect forcing them to quit? The answer is absolutely yes. However, forcing employees to quit for justified reasons is not actionable and therefore is still much better than simply firing them from most "Blue-Haired Ladies'" standpoint. Accordingly (as you should explain to the employees), the option of allowing them to quit is something that they may or may not want to have for future reference purposes, and they perhaps may want to avoid anything negative on their resumes.

Frequently, employees may inquire as to whether or not they'll be able to collect unemployment under such circumstances. Your response should be that you are not an expert, but it is your understanding that whether you are terminated versus being forced to quit does not determine unemployment eligibility. Rather such is determined on the reason you were either terminated or forced to quit.

For example, if an employee is drunk on the job and he is either terminated or forced to quit, it is most unlikely he will collect unemployment benefits no matter what. On the other hand, if an employee is terminated for simply being negligent on the job, most likely she will receive unemployment benefits whether she was forced to quit or was terminated. Do not in any manner mislead employees.

The realties are that again from a liability standpoint, (for you) it is significantly better for them to quit as opposed to being fired. However, you should not push this or force this upon them. Simply give them the choice.

It is conceivable during a termination that an employee may bring up some fact or issue that you were totally unaware of before the termination. If this occurs wherein you are blindsided, such means obviously you didn't exactly have your ducks in a row. In these very rare circumstances, you need to fall back to Step #6 and "buy time." In this type of a situation you would tell the employee: "I will have to get back to you." Obviously if this occurs, you have already substantially damaged the employer-employee relationship, and further it is certainly an indication to the employee that you as well as the company do not exactly have your act together. However, if you have done everything that you are required to do, you should not be engaged in a dialogue about the merits or lack thereof of a termination.

If this is a situation where you have decided that severance pay is justified, advise the individual as follows:

> "The company has decided, whether you decide to quit or be terminated, that they would like to provide some financial assistance to you and part as amicably as reasonably possible. To that end, the company has agreed to provide to you a severance-pay package conditioned upon you signing our standard agreement."

As it relates to his agreeing to sign the severance pay agreement, it is preferable to have him sign such immediately; however, this may not always be possible. Therefore if it's clear he is not going to agree to sign such then and there, give him the option of getting back to you on such within a short time frame (a matter of days). If you have a concern there might be an age discrimination claim, some jurisdictions mandate that he be permitted a number of days to consider, as well as a number of additional days to rescind the agreement, as well as the right to consult with legal counsel. Check with a qualified attorney (see Step #21).

After this has been accomplished, you then present to him the exit interview form (see Step #5). Remind him that pursuant to whatever policy section in your personnel handbook, he is required to fill out the form. Also make sure he turns over any keys, beeper, or other employer property at this time. Thereafter, provide to him his final paycheck and Cobra documentation (Cobra documentation are the forms that are to be filled out by employees who have health care benefits, wherein they are required to be provided notification of their right to continue health care benefits following the cessation of their employment. If you do not provide health care benefits, there is no requirement to provide such notification).

Additionally, at the end of the discussion, advise him (at his discretion) that he can remove his personal effects immediately. Tell him that either you or the other representative from the employer will assist him in that regard, or if he likes, he can come to the place of business on the following Saturday or some other mutually convenient non-working time and day to pick up his belongings. If the employee indicates that he does not need any assistance in removing his items, make it clear to him that it's a company policy that he is not permitted to be on the premises any further without an escort.

If for any reason the employee becomes confrontational and/or refuses to leave, do not engage in any form of self-help (i.e., forcibly dragging the employee out of the office by his ankles, etc.), but rather advise him that if he does not act reasonably or remove himself as you have requested, you will have to contact the legal authorities. If he continues to refuse, contact the legal authorities. On the other hand, if he becomes emotional and is simply too embarrassed to leave the meeting because he is afraid of who might see him, you should wait it out with him (which quite frankly creates rather long uncomfortable moments).

Under no circumstances ever force an employee out of such a meeting who is having emotional problems. At the same time, do not apologize in any manner for the terminating action, in that such can later be construed as an admission that you did not believe the termination was justified.

Also, if for whatever reason after you've gone through this entire procedure, the employee begs or pleads with you to provide to him some type of letter of recommendation, simply tell him that you will have to consider the matter and get back to him (i.e., buy time, per Step #9) (also see Section 5.7 regarding references). However, it is strongly recommended that you do not provide him any such reference or recommendation, in that it is inconsistent to provide such when you're firing somebody for performance reasons. This can later be used against you to attack your credibility.

If anything else comes up that was unsuspected during the termination itself, simply advise the employee that you have to consider the matter and get back to him (i.e., buy time, as set forth in Step #6).

Finally, at the end of this meeting, let the employee know that if he prefers, you can call somebody on his behalf to have him picked up, or if necessary that you can call a cab for him to take him home. While most employees under the circumstances will not accept such proposals, such offers are appropriate under the circumstances and quite frankly, if litigation later does ensue, you want to show that you were as reasonable as possible.

Throughout this meeting (which may last only a few minutes), if litigation does ensue, you will be questioned about such for literally hours. The employee's attorney will be asking you questions about every word, expression, emotion, reaction, and response that occurred during the meeting, and then typically ask you the same thing again in several different ways so as to determine your credibility. Be assured that it is most important you remember everything that took place during the meeting because the employee will remember it all in intimate detail. Consequently, in the litigation setting, when it gets down to the employee's credibility versus yours regarding what was said and done, it is imperative that you keep track of what was done and said. To testify in front of a "Blue-Haired Lady" that you simply don't remember comes across as not only uncaring but callous during what may well be the most emotional event in this individual's life.

It is for these reasons that I typically recommend that the persons on behalf of the employer who took part in the meeting do a joint memorandum of what all transpired during the meeting, to be prepared immediately after the meeting has occurred. If during the termination meeting, the employee requests that he be allowed to tape record the meeting, advise him "no." If he persists in doing the tape recording, advise him that the meeting is over and he is being terminated for violating company policies and procedures and that you have nothing further to say. Then thank him for his attendance at the meeting.

THE ORIGIN OF GETTING SACKED
Back in the old days, when employees worked in the factories they had to supply their own tools of the trade, which they often carried in bags or sacks. When an employer was getting rid of such an employee, they would hand to him his tool bag and tell him to get out, which in essence meant "getting sacked."

Section 10.4: Post Termination

After the individual has been terminated, it's not unusual for the person who is representing the employer, who has to walk the individual out to her car or pick up her belongings, to try and make the employee feel better or apologize to her. Do not under any circumstances allow that to occur. Frequently the employee, who is looking at the possibilities of litigation, will try and get some type of apology out of the employer's representatives; however, do not fall into that trap. If she tries and asks about any details, advise him that he is not permitted to discuss the matter any further.

"They can't get you for what you didn't say."
—Calvin Coolidge

Another issue that frequently arises after the termination is what should the other employees be told? The answer is "nothing." The termination of an employee's employment is a matter of his or her right of privacy. Accordingly, this should not be discussed with anyone who is not in a need-to-know position. Any and all inquires should be answered by telling the inquirers that this is a personnel matter and it is contrary to company policy to discuss such, unless you and the terminated employee reach some other mutually acceptable method.

In some instances, you may be involved in situations where the termination is of interest to the media, which typically is most unfortunate for the boss and/or supervisor. Having represented the media, it has been my experience that the successful media know their audience, and in most cases the audience of the media is, in large part, employees as opposed to bosses or supervisors. Since most employees are not thrilled about buying a newspaper that talks about anyone *properly* being fired or disciplined (with the exception of a few employees who are movie stars), generally, media coverage is slanted toward the employee in its presentation. In addition, these employees have rights of privacy even after the termination of their employment. Therefore I strongly recommend against bosses or employers talking to the media about any discipline, including termination, of an employee's employment.

Frequently when bosses or supervisors talk with third persons about a discipline that their employee received, the employee can come back and sue either the supervisor and/or the employer for violating the employee's right of privacy. More specifically, whatever happened with regard to the employment of the employee is a matter protected under the employee's right of privacy, and neither the boss nor the supervisor has a right to discuss such with third parties, including the media. In addition, many bosses and supervisors arguably give their version of what took place when an employee is disciplined, which can be viewed as being defamatory, and then there is a whole separate claim that can be brought against the boss or supervisor for making such representations. Remember, if a boss or supervisor is sued for a violation of right of privacy or defamation claim, they can be sued for damages for emotional distress, loss of wages as well as punitive damages. Some employees like to go to the media regarding their terminations so as to theoretically build up support for their case and/or make themselves look better to their friends and neighbors and/or prospective employers. Again, it has been my experience that this is not typically to the advantage of the employee in that frequently employers are willing to pay out more money for settlement with the understanding that there will be some type of confidentiality agreement prohibiting the employee from disclosing the terms of their settlement to the media.

Contrary to the belief of many bosses and supervisors, it has been my experience that most employees, when advised by legal counsel, do not want to go to the media until their case has actually been settled or a determination has been made by the judge or jury. More specifically, it is to an employee's advantage to try and use the threat of a cloud of going to the media over an employer's head so as to require the employer, especially in settlement situations, to pay additional amounts of money to keep the terms and conditions of a settlement confidential. Most employers would prefer not to have it broadcast by the media that they paid out any sums to settle any case where they were being accused of discrimination or harassment; and therefore accordingly, with some notable exceptions, usually bosses and supervisors do not have to worry that much about employees badmouthing their boss or supervisor to the media while a lawsuit is pending. Oftentimes as well, the employee's attorneys direct their clients not to say anything to the media during a pending lawsuit because of the fact that the quotes can be used against the employee by the employer, and therefore this situation does not arise that often where employers have to be concerned about such matters.

There are certainly circumstances where communicating with the media may be necessary, but it has been my experience that that is a very small minority of the cases; and therefore the response by the employer to the media is: "This is an employment matter and therefore cannot be commented upon." While on its face this may seem to be less than satisfactory, overall it is typically the best strategy. In those rare instances where you do want to provide additional information to the media, it should be done by way of a pre-prepared press release, reviewed by legal counsel.

SECTION 11.0

HAVING THE RIGHT PEOPLE ON BOARD

Section 11:1: Selecting Qualified Legal Counsel

Surprisingly, little information is provided to the public regarding and/or relating to the topic of selection of legal counsel. In most instances, it is based in large part upon advertisements, by whatever someone sees under a website or the yellow pages, or by word of mouth.

There is a publication available at law libraries referred to as Martindale-Hubbell. This publication is put out in North America providing a breakdown and listing of the ratings of attorneys based upon the opinions of the judges and attorneys from the attorney's geographic area. The highest rating an attorney can receive is an AV rating, followed thereafter by a BV rating or a CV rating. As it turns out, many attorneys elect not to receive any rating from Martindale-Hubbell because unless they have an AV rating, they have concerns that potential clients will view them as less than stellar. Consequently, many attorneys have no listing or rating whatsoever by Martindale-Hubbell. The publication in addition specifies the areas of expertise by the attorneys. Obviously it would not be particularly beneficial to have a criminal law attorney handling your employment matters or vice versa. Therefore it is quite important to look into the background of the attorneys and then of course follow up with the references that attorneys should be willing to provide to you relating to their experience and practice.

In Ted Rall's book entitled *Revenge of the Latchkey Kids*, he listed the warning signs of lawyers to watch out for, including the following:

- Advertises on matchbooks and daytime TV
- Has an 800 number that spells out "damages"
- Requires money up front "to cover me in case something happens"
- Charges under one hundred dollars an hour
- Has signed photo of Al Sharpton on office wall
- Has signed photo of O. J. Simpson on office wall
- Dates Marcia Clark
- Doesn't have the key for the hall restroom "because of a misunderstanding with the landlord"
- Uses Kinko's
- Wears bow tie, knit tie, bolo tie, or string tie
- Has phone book listings under different first and last names
- Claims that he cares
- Keeps framed diplomas from three Kuwaiti High Schools in office
- Has office in cruddy building and cruddy neighborhood
- Has snazzy office in upscale neighborhood
- Says, "These things take time."
- "I don't want to take your money."
- Has Bert Bacharach tunes piped into phone while you are on hold
- Has a picket line outside of office. (Exception: if pickets are cops, hire immediately.)

In addition to the foregoing, I have a few suggestions including the following:

- Contact the local County Bar Association. They can either directly or indirectly give you references for attorneys practicing in the area that you are seeking.

- Check with your local State Bar about a particular attorney to see whether or not he or she has any history of disciplinary action.

- Check with others in your business as to whom they use and whether or not they are satisfied or dissatisfied with their attorney.

- Once you have actually contacted the attorney who you might retain, ask for references and then check out those references.

- Contact the local judges in your community and ask them about whom they might recommend. Frequently judges will not provide this information but just as frequently they do.

- Always make sure you check out how many years the attorney has actually been practicing, as well as how many trials she has actually been involved with, and specifically what types of trials and cases she has handled in the past, as well as her rates and estimates for proving service to you.

> *"A lawyer is a man who gets two other men*
> *to take off their clothes and then*
> *he runs away with them."*
> —*Carl Sandburg*

> *"Never go to a doctor whose office plants have died."*
> —*Erma Bombeck*

Section 11:2: Human Resources

As to human resource professionals, unfortunately the field is quite diversified. In many instances, a human resources representative for most smaller companies is usually the office manager or someone else who just found out the day before that he is now in charge of human resources with no prior experience or background. Make sure that your company has someone designated to handle human resources as at least part of his duties and responsibilities if so as only to make sure that someone is going to take the responsibility for keeping updated on the changes and modifications to the laws in this ever-changing field.

These days, there are all types of institutions offering a variety of training and education on the topic of human resources. This ranges from night classes at local colleges or universities to private schools offering human resource programs as well as of course full college degrees.

Make sure, when seeking such a representative, that you follow the references in Step #4 regarding proper screening and interviewing (if you are like most mom-and-pop companies who cannot afford individuals with degrees in such areas, spend at least the $400.00 to $500.00 that it costs for a typical one-day training program that could save you literally hundreds of thousands of dollars for your HR representative). Remember, it is an ongoing process and all too often companies do not think to spend any effort or money on human resources until they get sued, and then it is too late.

Section 12.0

Avoiding Retaliation
and How to Cope

An area that has only been briefly touched upon so far in this book is the topic of retaliation. Most all jurisdictions have some law that prohibits bosses or supervisors from retaliating against employees for exercising their lawful rights. In many jurisdictions the law provides that if an employer's action, whether it be termination or some other form of discipline toward an employee, "is motivated" out of retaliation because of the employee's exercise of her own lawful rights, that such is a basis to sue for not only loss of wages, but also damages for emotional distress as well as punitive damages and, in some instances, arguably attorney's fees when the retaliation is based on discriminatory conduct as well.

Frequently, retaliation lawsuits are easier to recover by employees than are discrimination lawsuits in that for the most part, all that the employees need to show is that the retaliatory conduct is close in time to the exercise by the employees of their lawful conduct. The recovery again for retaliation claims can also be in the six- and seven-digit numbers, which is why in most all discrimination lawsuits that our firm handles, usually the employees are also suing for retaliation.

Examples of retaliation claims include employees who are terminated within a relatively short time frame after they filed a workers' compensation claim, gone on pregnancy leave, complained about not receiving overtime payments, complained about discrimination and/or sexual harassment, as well as any other unlawful conduct engaged in by the boss or supervisor. Keep in mind that any time an employee brings a claim against a particular boss or supervisor, that such in essence makes it very difficult for that boss or supervisor to be further involved in any such investigation on behalf of the company in that they are now tainted. That is why in many of these situations either a separate supervisor is brought in or perhaps even outside counsel, especially if the employee is complaining about the human resources department or representative.

This is one of the reasons why it is so important to make sure that before any action is taken toward an employee, that there is a paper trail (see Step #31). If you do have to take disciplinary action toward an employee who might well have complained about some action engaged in by the company, your only chance of prevailing on such a matter is to have a lengthy and detailed paper trail showing that the complaints about this person had occurred long before any complaints or whistle-blowing activities.

A Final Thought

It is certainly possible at this point in time that most bosses and supervisors who have read through this entire book are now placing a plastic bag over their heads while leaping off a tall bridge into a shallow pond.

It, however, continues to be the premise of this book that those situations for which you have been prepared or aware of are not going to be the most difficult. Rather it is those circumstances where you have been blind-sided that cause all the havoc.

Accordingly I do not agree with Bill Watterman in his cartoon *Calvin and Hobbes,* when they state: "The secret to enjoying your job is to have a hobby that is even worse." As set forth at the beginning of this book, it is and continues to be this author's view that working as a boss or supervisor is well worth all the trials and tribulations associated with having such a position. I for one would have it no other way. Keeping it all in perspective can make sure you are in a field that you enjoy. Remember, the people who are the best at their jobs are typically the people who enjoy what they are doing.

> *"When written in Chinese, the word 'crisis'*
> *is composed of two characters:*
> *one represents danger,*
> *the other represents opportunity."*
> —*John F. Kennedy*

ABOUT THE AUTHOR

Geoffrey Hopper began employment at the age of six working for his father's steel company located in California, working his way up through the family-owned steel fabrication business and obtaining his own steel fabricator's contractor's license as a teenager while at the same time going to college. He then graduated from law school by the age of twenty-four where he was selected as best oral advocate. From there he was employed by a prestigious law firm where he worked for nearly twenty years in litigation, during which time he also served as the president of California's Riverside County's Bar Association and began his practice in the area of employment and business law. Eventually this practice evolved into not only writing numerous articles but also providing in excess of 1,000 lectures and seminars for attorneys, law schools, universities, businesses, service organizations and clients. In 2001, he retired as a partner from that firm and started his own firm and now practices in Redlands, California, serving literally hundreds of employers in both labor and employment matters. He has been selected as one of the best attorneys in the United States as well as having received the highest independent rating available for attorneys in North America. He and his wife Lauralea have three children and reside in Lake Arrowhead, California.

ROBERT D. REED PUBLISHERS ORDER FORM

Call in your order for fast service and quantity discounts
(541) 347-9882

<u>OR</u> *order on-line at* **www.rdrpublishers.com** *using PayPal.*
<u>OR</u> *order by mail: Make a copy of this form; enclose payment information:*
Robert D. Reed Publishers
1380 Face Rock Drive, Bandon, OR 97411

<u>Note: Shipping is $3.50 1st book + $1 for each additional book.</u>

Send indicated books to:

Name _____

Address _____

City _____ State _____ Zip _____

Phone _____ Fax _____ Cell _____

E-Mail_____
Payment by check /__/ or credit card /__/ *(All major credit cards are accepted.)*

Name on card _____

Card Number_____

Exp. Date_____ Last 3-Digit number on back of card _____

	Qty.
Employment BS by Geoffrey Hopper $19.95	_____
100 Ways to Create Wealth by Steve Chandler & Sam Beckford $24.95	_____
The Small Business Millionaire by Steve Chandler & Sam Beckford $11.95	_____
Customer Astonishment by Darby Checketts $14.95	_____
Ten Commitments for Building High Performance Teams by Tom Massey. $11.95	_____
The Coming Widow Boom: What You and Your Loved Ones *Can Do to Prepare for the Unthinkable* by James F. "Buddy" Thomas, Jr. $14.95	_____

Other book title(s) from website:

_____ $ _____

_____ $ _____